Frank Talk

How YOU Can Make a Difference
In Your Career, Your Community, and
Your World Through Membership in
Rotary®

by

Frank J. Devlyn
Rotary International President, 2000-2001

with
David C. Forward

What Others Are Saying About *Frank Talk...*

"If enthusiasm and total commitment to Rotary's many causes is any judge of leadership, and a major reason to convince our business and professional friends to become members of Rotary, then Frank Devlyn stands out as an example of what Rotary is all about.

His book highlights that our motto *Service Above Self* has benefits to those we serve and rewards far beyond our imagination as Rotarians."

—A.H.R. (ROYCE) ABBEY, President, Rotary International, 1988-89

"When you read *Frank Talk*, you feel immediately that the Rotary pin this outstanding author is wearing on his lapel gives the following message:

I am reliable
I am available
I listen to you
I give more than I take
I add value

Thank you, Frank Devlyn, for your excellent book."

—ROBERT R. BARTH, President, Rotary International, 1993-94

"Only once in human history have we witnessed the total eradication of a dreaded disease, and that was smallpox more than two decades ago. Now the world stands on the brink of a second triumph—eradicating polio—and we have come to this point because of a global partnership in which Rotary International has played a leading role since 1985.

Because of the vast immunization campaign that Rotarians have helped sustain, the lives of millions of children have been, and will yet be, spared. I firmly believe the world will be polio free by 2005, thanks in large part to the Rotarians throughout the world and the leadership of Frank Devlyn.

I have no doubt that when the history of this crusade is written, the heroic contributions of Rotary International will loom large indeed."

—CAROL BELLAMY, Executive Director, UNICEF—United Nations Children's Fund

"Frank Devlyn's tremendous enthusiasm and belief that Rotary is the most important humanitarian organization in the world, and his understanding that the more Rotarians, the greater the work, has been contagious in bringing in many new members. He has truly "Created Awareness" of our need and "Taken Action." This man of vision and dynamic leadership has been invaluable to the future of Rotary, and it has been an honor and privilege to serve with him."

—HERBERT G. BROWN, President, Rotary International, 1995-96

"I have known Frank Devlyn for 30 years. During that time, I have watched with interest and pride as he developed from a young entrepreneur to an international business leader. At the same time, I have seen him grow from a new Rotarian to world president of Rotary. Frank has found through Rotary the secret of how to find more friends and at the same time a way to serve humanity. In our country of Mexico, he is one of our most respected leaders, and he credits Rotary for much of his personal and professional growth. *Frank Talk* is the story that will show you what Rotary can do in your life, also."

—Dr. CARLOS CANSECO, President, Rotary International, 1984-85

"Frank Devlyn's book brings to each one of us a fuller understanding of what Rotary stands for. The Rotary Emblem was first a wheel of commerce, then a wheel of industry, and now is a wheel of hope. Rotary brings hope: for children without polio, for food for all people, for a life worth living, for a world at peace. *Frank Talk* shows why everyone should join Rotary to bring hope to others and make a difference in their community."

—M.A.T. CAPARAS, President, Rotary International, 1986-87

"For all the joy we receive from serving others less fortunate, for all the happiness we each gain from the friends we make in Rotary, those rewards can be multiplied if we bring in new members. *Frank Talk* is a refreshing, entertaining book that goes a long way toward that goal. It shows readers why *we* joined Rotary, and why we stay. It shows the non-Rotarians the inner satisfaction we Rotarians get from serving others, because no matter what our race, creed or religion, to Rotarians, *Mankind is our Business.*"

—RICHARD D. KING, President, Rotary International, 2001-02

"I have known Frank Devlyn since 1974 and we have built a wonderful friendship as we served together through Rotary. I commend Frank's willingness to improve Rotary, and these pages show his ideals and reflect his enthusiasm. Thank you, Frank, for your friendship and your service to Rotary and humanity."

—LUIS VICENTE GIAY, President, Rotary International, 1996-97

"In his own special way, as the successful business leader that he is, Frank Devlyn demonstrates that we are the guardians, each one of us. Every Rotarian individually is a guardian of the Rotary dream. We are the ones who have to take the lead in reaffirming those timeless values of dignity, decency, humanity and restraint. We are the integrating force so needed in the world."

—BILL HUNTLEY, President, Rotary International, 1994-95

"*Frank Talk* provides a fresh answer to a century-old question, 'Why Rotary?' Enjoy Frank Devlyn's personalized answer to this question, which more than 3,000,000 men and women worldwide have pondered."

—CHARLES C. KELLER, President, Rotary International, 1987-88

"*Frank Talk* is a wonderful resource for Rotarians to give to their friends, business associates, and community leaders. It shows that person in the street who doesn't understand what Rotary is or what Rotarians do why they should join this 1.2-million person world fellowship of people committed to making a difference in the world."

—JAMES LACY, President, Rotary International, 1998-99

"Frank Devlyn is very cognizant of the potential that Rotary has to promote better understanding and goodwill among the peoples of all nations. During his presidency he has launched numerous programmes—concrete actions—to help the 1.2 million members in almost 200 countries achieve that goal. Rotary has, for almost 100 years extended humanitarian service wherever Rotarians are found. After reading *Frank Talk* you will want to become a part of this global forum for peace at the dawning of the new millennium."

—BHICHAI RATTAKUL, President, Rotary International, 2002-2003

"*Frank Talk* is a vivid document telling us what Rotary is all about and what we can achieve, each in a different way. The lives of millions of suffering people are being improved every day through the tireless efforts of Rotarians who act with "Consistency, credibility, and continuity."

—CARLO RAVIZZA, President, Rotary International, 1999-2000

"When Frank talks, he talks frankly, and with great enthusiasm, for he has seen what Rotary does to change peoples' lives. But more importantly, he has seen what Rotary cannot do because of the limitation on its resources—especially its human resources; hence his crusade to invite others into Rotary membership, to share his enthusiasm and to experience the satisfaction which comes from selfless service to others."

—CLEM RENOUF, President, Rotary International, 1978-79

"*Frank Talk* reflects the dedication, commitment, and vision of a man who has seen and experienced Rotary as an enthusiastic worker, an ardent follower, and a dynamic leader. Frank Devlyn is a man in a hurry, a storehouse of energy, always on the move and carrying the world with him. He has aggressive sincerity—yet a refreshing common touch in his thoughts, words, and deeds.

This book shows how a busy person can find time for the good of the community and of humanity. It has been a joy getting to know Frank—and I'm sure you will feel the same after reading *Frank Talk*."

—RAJENDRA K. SABOO, President, Rotary International, 1991-92

"Frank Devlyn is a world leader who through Rotary helped people throughout the world have a better life. His enthusiasm for programs of Rotary is a strong motivating force to increase membership so that there will be more Rotarians available to help even more people."

—WILLIAM E. SKELTON, President, Rotary International, 1983-84

Frank Talk

How YOU Can Make a Difference
In Your Career, Your Community, and
Your World Through Membership in
Rotary®

by

Frank J. Devlyn
Rotary International President, 2000-2001

with

David C. Forward

This book has been produced by Frank Devlyn at no cost whatsoever to
Rotary International. All proceeds from the sale of *Frank Talk* will be donated
to The Rotary Foundation and designated for avoidable blindness projects.

ReachForward Publishing Group
www.ReachForward.com

FRANK TALK

How YOU Can Make a Difference: In Your Career, Your Community, and Your World Through Membership in Rotary

For information address:
Frank J. Devlyn
Rotary International
One Rotary Center
1560 Sherman Avenue
Evanston, IL 60201, USA.

ROTARY®, . and are trademarks of Rotary International. Used with permission.

Printed in the United States of America
Cover and Biography photo by B. Aetin Haig. Used with permission.
Cover design and layout: Ad Graphics, Inc., Tulsa, OK

This book is not an official publication of Rotary International.

FRANK TALK may be purchased individually for $12.95 or at substantial discounts for bulk orders of 10 or more copies. Rates are quoted in US funds and do not include shipping and handling.

For more information see the Resource Center at:
www.ReachForward.com
www.FrankDevlyn.org.
Phone: + 1.856.988.1738
Fax: + 1.856.988.0511

First printing June 2001
Second printing July 2001

Library of Congress Number: 2001117406

ISBN: 0-9711030-0-3

This book is dedicated to two persons. First, to Antonio Joannis, a dedicated Rotarian from my home state of Chihuahua, Mexico, who went out of his way to recommend both me and my brother Jesse as prospective members to a Rotarian friend in the distant city of Mexico City, 1,200 kilometers away.

Second, it was that Rotarian, Emilio Sanchez Chavez, who didn't know us personally, who after hearing the recommendation from a fellow Rotarian took the time to explain the significance of Rotary to me 31 years ago and then sponsored me into the Rotary Club of Anahuac-Mexico City. I shall forever be indebted to him for seeing in me something that he thought made me worthy as a Rotarian, and pledge to return the favor to others as long as I may live.

—Frank

ACKNOWLEDGMENTS

When I first suggested the idea of a book that would tell the story of what it means to be a Rotarian, many people said it was a great idea. Then when I moved forward with it in early March, just as many folks told me I was crazy: *it is impossible to write a book in a month!*

But Rotarians are somewhat used to being told they cannot achieve the impossible, then prove the doubters wrong when they call upon the vast supply of talented, motivated members within our organization. That's how I accomplished the task of this book, and I must begin by thanking some of them.

Of course, without the unfailing love and support of my wife, Gloria Rita and daughters Melanie, Stephanie, and Jennifer, I could never have become world president of Rotary International. I hope they know how much I love them and appreciate them.

I am grateful to Lou Piconi, vice president of Rotary International and past-director, T. D. Griley, who served as my aide during my presidential year. It was the two of them who said of this book idea: "Let's make it happen!"

I also thank David C. Forward, an internationally-known writer and public speaker for his help in writing and producing *Frank Talk* in record time. David is a member of the Rotary Club of

Marlton, New Jersey, and I'm also grateful to his fellow club members Ron Lynch and Bud Umbaugh for their suggestions. We appreciate the professional editorial advice from Jo Nugent, former associate editor of *The Rotarian* magazine, who is now a member of the Rotary Club of Spearfish, South Dakota. I also wish to thank Jim Weems, a member of the Rotary Club of Tulsa, Oklahoma, whose company, Ad Graphics, did such a superb job designing the cover and printing the book. My Webmaster, Harriett Schloer, of the Rotary Club of Bend, Oregon, also provided many hours of valuable service in adding the book to the Website and designing promotional materials for that medium.

To the Rotary International Board of Directors, the Secretariat staff, and my many friends who helped me not only with this book, but also throughout my 31-year love affair with Rotary, please accept the heartfelt thanks of a humble and grateful man. *Muchas gracias!*

—**Frank J. Devlyn**

CONTENTS

About Frank Devlyn

The story of Frank Devlyn is that of a young man who grew up on the border cities of Ciudad Juarez, Chihuahua, Mexico and El Paso, Texas. Frank Devlyn is a truly bilingual and bicultural person. He has had the unique opportunity to live, work, and study on both sides of the border. While working at his family's small optical store in Juarez, Frank studied at the University of Texas at El Paso, and earned degrees from the Graduate School of Business at the Instituto Panamericano de Alta Direccion de Empresas in Mexico and the School of Optometry of the Mexican Association of Opticians and Optometrists.

At the age of 22, due to the death of his father, Frank found himself as the head of the small family optical business. Though hard work, study, and with the help of his mother and brothers, Jesse and Patrick, Frank grew the family business into one of the world's largest optical chains. Devlyn Optical currently consists of over four hundred optical stores, a chain of wholesale optical suppliers and laboratories, and a chain of eye care surgical centers. His story is one of remarkable success in business and beyond. Frank Devlyn occupies the highest levels of leadership in an array of business, professional, and civic organizations.

Frank is a past president of Mexico's National Association of Opticians and Optometrists, past president of the Optical Division of the National Chamber of Industries, past president of the Mexico City Toastmaster's Club, and past president of the Association of Hearing Aid Distributors in Mexico. He is a national board member of the Mexican Red Cross, global board member of Goodwill Industries, serves on the Board of Directors for the Wheelchairs for the World Foundation, and treasurer of the Mexican Tuberculosis Association. He has served on the Board of Directors for the Young Men's Christian Association (YMCA) of Mexico City, the National Pro Blind Association and the National Mexican Association of Public and Private Administration. He is a national adviser for the Mexican Government's commission of health to the handicapped and serves on the boards of the National Bank of Mexico and the Inverlat Bank.

Frank is also a devoted family man. He is the respected head of one of the best-known families in Mexico with his wife, Gloria Rita. Frank's daughters, Melanie, Stephanie, and Jennifer, and his grandchildren, play a significant role in his life. Even with his many business and professional commitments, Frank remains at heart a committed and devoted husband, father, and grandfather.

A Rotarian since 1970, Frank is a member of the Rotary Club of Anahuac in Mexico City. He is founding editor of the regional magazine *Rotarismo en Mexico*, and has served The Rotary Foundation as a trustee and Rotary International as director, international assembly discussion group leader, committee chairman and member, and district governor. In the world of Rotary, Frank Devlyn has occupied almost every position on the club, district, and international levels, rising to the position of the President of Rotary International in 2000-2001. The Rotary Foundation bestowed on Frank the Distinguished Service Award and Citation for Meritorious Service in recognition of his support for its international humanitarian and educational programs. Having completed his term as Rotary International president, Frank was appointed to lead the Task Force on Avoidable Blindness.

FOREWORD

It was over a decade ago, that I recall strolling along the broad streets of Monterrey, Mexico. We talked about Rotary, and our families, and some philosophy of life. It was an opportunity to get to know Frank Devlyn in a way I had never seen him before. We had, of course, been long time friends in Rotary and served on several committees and special Rotary assignments. On this day he talked quietly, as he sometimes does. He had serious dreams to be fulfilled. He had ideas, yet to be refined. He had a message that morning, but he had a very small audience, too. It was during that morning, as we walked and talked together, that I realized Frank was destined to become the world leader of Rotary International—some day.

This book is the opportunity to have a glimpse of the deepest thoughts of that very rare Rotarian.

I first met Frank Devlyn in the early 1970's, when a Rotary committee assignment brought us together. He was impressive. He had everything going for him—tall, energetic, fluent in several languages, beautiful family, and all the prerequisites of a very successful businessman.

Added to these personal attributes, Frank seemed to have discovered that the basic tenets of Rotary could easily be applied to one's professional, community and family life.

Our paths crossed more and more often, and I watched as he tackled any challenge with tireless energy and creative imagination. There was no task in Rotary too small for him. He would respond to any call for action. He is the kind of person who doesn't just <u>belong</u> to a Rotary Club; he actually <u>lives</u> Rotary.

As the years passed, we met at various Rotary International functions, Frank and Gloria Rita would share stories of their three beautiful daughters, their growing family optical business, the new joy of becoming grandparents, and newly found experiences in Rotary. He is devoted to his family, and considers hundreds of Rotarians part of his extended family. I am sure that Frank Devlyn has never met a stranger. He immediately involves everyone in conversation. This happens in every part of the world.

As I observed Frank assume assignments on the R.I. Board of Directors and later as a Trustee of The Rotary Foundation, it was evident that his successful business experiences were applicable to Rotary's concern for membership expansion, effective public relations, and promoting active projects of service. Frank seems fearless in taking on new tasks. He seems always to demonstrate exceptional skills of motivation and inspiration whether talking with prospective Rotarians or challenging aging clubs.

As the world President of Rotary International, Frank initiated a proactive team of twenty Task Forces, which gave Rotary new levels of humanitarian activity in avoidable blindness, jobs for disabled persons, children at risk, crime and violence prevention, population and development, and other world community services. In addition, he has led Rotary into the amazing world of Internet communication and information exchange. As is customary, Frank does everything in a big way.

As part of his emphasis on membership development, he decided to leave a legacy to help introduce more members into the wonderful world of Rotary. This was the beginning of *Frank Talk*.

Even before the first copies rolled off the presses, advance orders signaled that *Frank Talk* was going to be a best seller. No Rotary funds were used to produce this book, and yet he decided to donate every penny of the proceeds to The Rotary Foundation. All funds will support avoidable blindness projects, one of Frank's premiere interests.

Frank Talk is fun to read. It is a typical Frank Devlyn experience, through and through! It tells the story of Frank running into three other people and how he invited them to join and enjoy Rotary. The answers they give and the excuses they recite, are typically ones that you hear over and over again. But, as you can imagine, Frank debunks the stereotypical myths, and shows his new friends that the benefits of joining Rotary far outweigh any minor objections they have for not wishing to change their lives by becoming Rotarians.

Frank Talk is a wonderful book for Rotarians to read to keep their internal fires burning. More importantly, it is a valuable resource for Rotarians to give to prospective members, guest speakers or local community leaders. In a wonderful way, the book tells what Rotary is, what Rotary does, and why joining a Rotary club will enrich your life.

It is a book you will enjoy reading and sharing with your friends who should know the real Frank Devlyn and the value of Rotary membership.

—**Clifford L. Dochterman**
President, Rotary International, 1992-93
Moraga, California, U.S.A.
June 2001

INTRODUCTION

On a bitterly cold night in February 1905, a young lawyer named Paul P. Harris went to dinner with his new friend Silvester Schiele. Silvester was just about his *only* friend in the big city of Chicago, and so Paul was very lonely. He had grown up in the tiny Vermont village of Wallingford, where everybody knew one another, where one's word was one's bond and where merchants and customers greeted one another by name. Because of family circumstances, he had been raised by his grandparents, and they had taught him to be tolerant, respectful, hardworking, and honest. When he graduated from law school and arrived in the teeming metropolis of America's second-largest city, he was utterly shocked at what he found.

His grandparents were now dead, he had no stable family homestead to return to, and Chicago was as different from Wallingford as night is from day. In those days there were no consumer protection laws—in fact, the *only* law was *caveat emptor*—let the buyer beware. Corruption was rife; employees and customers suffered at the hands of unscrupulous businesses; but most of all, Paul missed the fellowship he had experienced in his formative years. In Wallingford, if the family ran short of money, the grocer would willingly extend credit; neighbors wouldn't hesitate to bring food over when someone was sick, and if a child was walking home and a storm sprang up, the closest family would take him in and care for him until it abated.

Paul proposed an idea to Silvester. Why not gather together a group of businesspeople who could meet regularly for fellowship, and who could exchange ideas of mutual help? They would restrict membership to one representative from each line of business or profession, their rationale being that if many people from one type of business were members, they would likely sit around and "talk shop" with one another—hardly conducive to the camaraderie that Paul envisioned.

Four people showed up at the first meeting: a coal merchant, a tailor, a mining engineer—and Paul Harris, the lawyer. At the next meeting, those four brought along a printer, an organ manufacturer, and a real estate broker. At each subsequent meeting new members were introduced, and the venue rotated from one member's place of business to another, hence the choice of the name *Rotary* Club.

Rotary soon expanded across America and then throughout the world. Within a very few years, Rotarians changed the focus of their organization from one of friendship and business exchange to one of *service*. As the world's first service club, Rotary reached out to serve:

- The local community, as a way of giving back to the neighborhoods that patronized their businesses.

- Internationally, with programs that encourage peace and the relief of suffering.

- Through their vocations—with Rotarians taking the leading role in creating a Code of Business Ethics which thousands of businesses adopted.

- Children, whom Rotarians taught job skills, and provided countless opportunities for those with disabilities.

Rotary's expansion around the world attracted kings, princes, and political, religious, and community leaders of all types into fellowship with businessmen and professionals. But Paul's original reason for starting Rotary was never forgotten. When men of high office sit down at the table with the corner shopkeeper in Rotary, titles disappear. It is no longer "Prince" this or "Doctor" that, but "Larry" and "Tom." Rotary was—and is—an organization that strives to remove barriers, believing that a group of dedicated, intelligent, influential men and women—imbued with the spirit of voluntary service—can change the world for good. To some Rotarians that means getting their hands dirty on a Saturday morning while building a wheelchair ramp at the local library. To others, it means writing a check to buy a computer for an inner city school. To yet others, it means hosting a Rotary exchange student in their home or traveling to Bangladesh to provide a well that will supply a village with clean drinking water.

Rotary is an organization that is truly international, apolitical, and without any specific religious or denominational affiliations. And it *has* changed the world for the better. Rotarians helped broker a peace pact between warring South American countries, helped found UNESCO, and launched the PolioPlus campaign to eradicate the scourge of polio from the face of the earth by 2005.

But Rotary's roots remain in the men and women who attend their local club meetings for fun and fellowship, while committed to the joy of serving those less fortunate.

I am one such member. I grew up with one foot in my father's homeland, the United States, and one in the land of my mother—Mexico. I saw first hand the benefits to all concerned when people of differing cultures and nationalities put aside their differences and prejudices and sought to better understand one another. My Dad and Mom were optometrists and they started a retail optical store in our hometown of Ciudad Juarez. From the age of nine I loved to work in the optical shop after school. It was as if I left my classroom of academia to study in the classroom of life, for it was here that I watched my parents treat their customers with dignity, integrity, and friendship. I knew from an early age that I wanted to choose the same profession and to give something back to the community that gave my family its livelihood.

After graduating from college, I went to work alongside my mother and father in the family business. Soon my brothers Jesse and Pat joined us, and we began to expand Devlyn Optical. I became active in professional associations, rising to the presidency of Mexico's National Association of Opticians and Optometrists, and several other organizations. My father died when I had just turned 22. We had seven optical stores at the time, and we decided that what had been the dream he shared with me would now become the family dream, and we grew the business both horizontally and vertically. We opened stores all over the country and expanded into the manufacture and distribution of optical products. But there is more to life than market share and a comfortable income. I just didn't know what it was that I was missing at the time.

In 1970, I was invited to join the Rotary Club of Anahuac in Mexico City. I knew Rotary was—and remains—a very prestigious organization. It is the crown jewel of service clubs, and my life has never been the same since I became a Rotarian. From the hundreds of responses that other Rotarians have submitted to my website, www.FrankDevlyn.org, (see Appendix A), I am not alone in feeling that way.

I freely admit now that "prestige" was probably not the most worthy reason for me to have joined a service club. But at least it got me to join! I was not disappointed, either. I have met some of the world's most interesting leaders as a result of my involvement in Rotary. Not long after I joined, I attended the 75th anniversary celebration of the Rotary Club of Mexico City and found myself—a young rank-and-file new Rotarian—chatting away with Luis Echeveria, the then-president of Mexico, who was the guest speaker.

While "prestige" and "business connections" may have been my reasons for *joining* Rotary, I soon discovered the real rewards of membership. The first is friendship. I have made friends on every continent on earth as a direct result of Rotary. As a new member, I noticed that when Rotarians get together, they feel a genuine bond of friendship, whether it is when a member visits another club in a nearby town or when Rotarians of one country meet others from a different part of the globe. People from all over the world have stayed in my home, and my wife and I have been invited as guests when we travel overseas. Paul Harris had on the wall of his office a framed quotation from his favorite poet, Ralph Waldo Emerson: *He who has a thousand friends has not a friend to spare.* I probably have thousands of friends today, and I met the vast majority of them through Rotary.

As I became more active in my club, they made me a club officer, and then club president. I was very fortunate to go on to become district governor and to be elected to the Board of Directors of Rotary International. From the very beginning of my membership in Rotary, my circle of friends grew larger, and my family enjoyed the work Rotary does and the people who do it. My wife, Gloria Rita, made friends with Rotarians and their spouses all over the world, as did my daughters, all of whom traveled with me to district conferences and international conventions. All three of my brothers have long since joined Rotary, and my mother is an honorary Rotarian. They each have told me on many occasions how proud they are of the work that Rotary does and of our family's very small part in that work. On July 1, 2000, I became only the third person from Mexico to serve as world president of Rotary International.

For two years—one as president-elect and one as president—I have traveled the world, seemingly in a different city every day. People frequently ask me, "How do you do it? Aren't you permanently exhausted?" Of course it does become tiring, with so many flights back and forth across multiple time zones. But without fail, every time I felt tired as I got ready to go to another conference or meeting, as sure as the sun rises in the east, I would be reminded of what this Rotary idea is all about. That invigorated me! What an energizing sensation to hear such compelling testimony from so many people.

Total strangers would tell me how they had been Rotary Foundation scholars and now use Rotary's principles as their daily guide in their important positions in government and industry. I'd see people enthusiastically serving the old, the young, the sick, the poor, and the blind. I saw Rotary projects that provided artificial limbs to landmine victims at the cost of a mere $100. I saw Rotarian doctors—and their medical friends—travel at their own expense to faraway countries where they repaired cleft palates, straightened crippled legs, and restored the sight of people who had given up hope of being "normal." I've seen projects that empower women to start their own businesses in developing countries through microcredit.

Rotary today merges its diversity and prestige with the expertise of partners to leverage our commitment to service even further. The biggest example of this partners-in-service concept is our relationship with the World Health Organization (WHO), the Centers for Disease Control, UNICEF, and ministries of health the world over. Together, we have been able to eradicate polio from entire continents—an accomplishment that none of us could have achieved alone. We are partnering with CBM International, Sightsavers, and others on avoidable blindness programs, with Goodwill Industries to give jobs to people with disabilities, and with the Wheelchairs Foundation to provide wheelchairs to everyone in the world who needs one. This is where Rotary's prestige is so helpful. If a Rotary club in Canada received a request for support from the Gulbarga Institute in India, they might throw it in the trash. But when they get a letter from the Gulbarga Rotary Club, saying they have partnered with the Institute and need support for their project—the Canadian Rotarians are more likely to help.

When I went to New York to present UN Secretary-General Kofi Annan with an award for his polio eradication efforts, he told the audience, "If anyone should be recognized, it should be the UN that recognizes Rotary—not only for what you've done for the worldwide eradication of polio, but for how you've helped in 30,000 communities around the world."

As Rotary approaches its 100th birthday, it is not a doddering centenarian, it is more active, alive, and relevant than it has ever been. One Rotarian I met—a doctor with 49 years of perfect attendance at his club—told me, "One of my greatest contributions to Rotary was made 30 years ago when I brought that young lady," he pointed to the club president, "into the world."

Now she—and you, and I—have an even greater opportunity to bring life into the world. The new peace scholarships that The Rotary Foundation just launched will train graduate students in peacemaking and conflict resolution in major universities around the world. That means the money I give to the Rotary Foundation today could equip a person tomorrow to help two fighting nations to end a war that is costing a million human lives. Rotarians in the developed world are already teaching entrepreneurship to people in emerging democracies, and it is no exaggeration to say that every minute of every day Rotarians are using their influence, their hands, and their generosity to make this world a better place for *all* of humankind.

Yet for all the good that Rotary does, for all the prestige the organization has, for all the fun we have at our meetings, why are there not more of us? If 1.2 million Rotarians do *this much* good, just imagine how much better our communities and the world beyond them would be if there were 2 million Rotarians. It is not an organization for everyone, just for those who are the best in their field.

The sad truth is that many people have not joined Rotary either because they don't know what it is, or because they have a wrong impression of it. That's an image problem that goes way back. Some people are still reluctant to join Rotary because of their perception that we are an all-male bastion—a boring old men's club that insists on them attending every meeting and which would cost them a fortune. Once again, I protest! That is all simply not true.

But the biggest reason why good people don't join Rotary is that we Rotarians don't ask them to. Oh sure, we ask our sons and daughters, our close business associates and friends to join sometimes, but we so often don't even think of our duty as advocates with most people we run across in our daily lives. That doctor I met who had brought his club president into the world has, in 49 years of Rotary membership only introduced one new member into his club. He told me he had delivered about 1,000 babies in his career. I think at least 10 percent of them would have been excited, elated and deeply honored—just like his club president was— if the doctor who brought them into this world had invited them many years later to join Rotary. What a missed opportunity.

Last year, I visited my father's hometown in Gilman, Illinois. I met the 28-year-old manager of a restaurant who manages 16 employees—she didn't even know what Rotary was. When I bought flowers to place on my grandmother's grave I asked the husband and wife who own the local floral shop about Rotary. They had never been invited to join the Rotary club because 30 years ago there was already a florist in the Gilman Rotary Club and long after he passed away, the club members forgot to fill his classification with another florist. Another missed opportunity.

I had a 90-minute meeting with Bill Gates, Senior, father of the Bill Gates of Microsoft. We talked about Rotary's programs and especially PolioPlus, for which I thanked him for his support. Bill was very interested in knowing about the work Rotary does, in fact, Rotary's good work is one of the reasons the Gates Foundation has given $50 million to eradicate polio. Then I asked him, "Bill, how come you never joined Rotary?" He told me, "I've never been asked!" I invited him to join right there—and he accepted. I asked the same question of Ken Behring, one of America's leading philanthropists, and founder of the Wheelchairs Foundation. And again, to the Prime Minister of Trinidad. In both those cases—and numerous others—they gave the same answer: "Nobody ever invited me to join." I asked them if they would accept *my* invitation and they were honored to join. Now you tell me how much better your Rotary club would be if it had a Bill Gates or Ken Behring or Prime Minister—or even the florist and restaurant manager—among its members.

That's why I wrote this book. As my presidential year was ending, I wanted to discuss in a conversational way what Rotary can do for *you*, and at the same time, what you can do for Rotary. I wrote this for existing Rotarians as a tool for them to give to prospective members. I wrote this for the non-Rotarians to repay the debt I owe to the man who invited me to join Rotary. You could be the next outstanding representative in your field who joins a local Rotary club initially because of how it will help you in business. Even if that is your primary reason for joining, I know you, like me, will soon make some of the best friends you will ever have. Then you will discover the inner joy that comes from lending a hand at a community service project; then perhaps you'll get involved in an international project—and, like me, and 1.2 million others, you'll be hooked! Our Code of Ethics that calls for open disclosure in all our dealings compels me to tell you this up front!

Over and over again, Rotarians on every continent have told me, "I joined a Rotary club and it made me a better person." "I became a Rotarian and my self-esteem went up." "I joined because I thought I could do something for others, but I've received back so much more than I've given."

I hope you'll join me as *Frank Talk* recounts the story of a recent trip in which four of us started as strangers and ended as partners in the journey of life—through Rotary.

—**Frank Devlyn**
Evanston, Illinois, USA.
June 2001

The Poona School & Home For the Blind required a bus to transport the blind girls from their hostel to the secondary school about five kilometers away. They used to commute by local transport bus, which was unsafe & uncomfortable. We decided to donate a bus under a matching grant program of The Rotary Foundation. Fortunately Rotarian Ken Rawlings of the Rotary Club of Eastbourne, United Kingdom, was in Pune. We discussed a project with him and he in turn presented it to Rotarian Hap Mills of the Rotary Club of Stuart, Florida. These two clubs along with the Rotary Clubs of Stuart Sunrise & Rotary Club of Hobe Sound / Port Salerno arranged a finance of $3,165. The Rotary Foundation was requested to match the contribution of $6,330. The bus was donated on 12th April. The girls were very happy, especially after learning that it also has a tape recorder. I have received a letter from one of the girls in Braille addressed to R.I. President Frank Devlyn in which it is written that they will not be able to see us but every time they travel in the bus they will remember Rotary. This was certainly a touching & memorable experience. This really reflects on the Internationality of our great organisation as five clubs across three continents came together for this project.

—Achyut Gokhale, Club President
Rotary Club of Pune Shivajinagar
Pune, Maharashtra,India

Rotary clubs from around the world quickly responded with disaster relief to victims of Hurricane Mitch which wreaked destruction on Honduras in 1999.

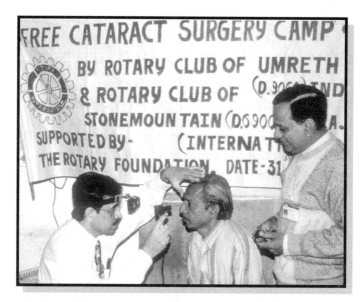

This Rotary club in India was a pioneer in Rotary's campaign for avoidable blindness, which for $100, can provide surgery that restores the sight to three people.

CHAPTER 1

Chance Encounter

D ense fog enveloped the airport like a giant gray shroud. Mighty jetliners—aeronautical arrows normally capable of connecting continents in a single bound—sat lifeless on the ramp, the paralyzed victims of the blanket of gloom. Pilots could not even see the ground from their cockpit windows. Nothing was moving. Not trucks. Not my flight. Not me.

The lines at the customer service counter snaked beyond the gate area and along the concourse like a motionless conga line. My final destination in the nation's capital was but a 50-minute flight away, and I had to be there for a gala event at which I was the keynote speaker that very evening. It was time to call for help. It was time to call RITS—Rotary International Travel Service—at the Rotary headquarters in Evanston, Illinois.

Within five minutes they had my solution all planned. "There's an express train that leaves in 48 minutes," the agent said, assuringly. "You need to get a cab to the main station downtown, and I've arranged for your ticket to be ready at the Will-Call window. You'll still have two hours between when the train arrives and when the dinner starts."

I hurried to the nearest exit door and turned right, thinking that the best spot to hail a taxi would be at the point where they entered the airport. As if in answer to my prayer, a cab appeared through the lingering mist.

"Taxi!"

"Taxi!"

"Taxi!"

It stopped right beside me, and as I reached for the door I turned to see the source of the multiple calls. Barely ten paces behind me, a woman was running in my direction. Three steps behind her was a young man with a pained look on his face.

"I've been trying to find a cab for 20 minutes," the woman protested. "My flight was cancelled and I have to get to the station to catch a train. I'm desperate! You're not heading into town by any chance, are you?"

"Better than that," I assured her. "I'm also going to the station. Hop in." The young man was now beside us. "Me too," he said. "Any chance you could make room for one more?"

As we pulled away from the curb, I got my first look at the hordes of passengers outside the terminal's main doors. There must have been a thousand people, all looking expectantly for a car, a bus, a cab—any form of transport that could move them closer to their destination. I turned to my guests. "Hi! I'm Frank Devlyn," I said, extending my hand.

"My name is Sue; I'm happy to meet you. And thank you so much for letting me share your taxi." She was an attractive woman, smartly dressed in a well-cut red suit with elegant accessories. Probably in her late-forties, I thought.

"I'm Bob. Pleased to meet you. Thanks for the ride." The man's introduction interrupted my inspection of Sue. He was much younger, maybe 30. He was dressed in neatly pressed blue jeans and a sweatshirt.

I enjoy studying human behavior. I like to try to understand what makes people act the way they do, so as the car sped along, I tried to unobtrusively observe my two guests. They could not have been more different. Sue was gregarious, funny, and warm. She freely used hand gestures when talking and was obviously one of those people who made friends easily. Bob, on the other hand, seemed to be the quiet type who rarely initiated conversation, and responded with monosyllabic answers.

They made quite a pair, I thought to myself. I spend so much time on airplanes that I sometimes try to guess what people do for a living, just by observing how they dress and behave. "I'll bet she is in public relations, and he is...hmmm...he might be an engineer, or one of those dot-com Generation Xers I've been meeting over the last couple of years," I silently speculated.

"Tell me about yourselves," I invited.

Probably to nobody's surprise, Sue spoke first. "I'm married and have two beautiful daughters, aged 19 and 22," she began. "For the past 25 years,

I've worked in the airline industry, for South American Airways." She went on to explain how she had worked her way up from junior sales representative to regional sales manager and it was clear she loved her job. But a few months earlier, the company had found itself in dire financial straits. It closed offices, eliminated routes, and laid off staff around the world. As a 25-year veteran, Sue's income made an attractive target for the cost-cutters at headquarters. They figured one way to restore the company to profitability was to offer early retirement to long-term employees, and Sue suddenly found herself a retiree— even if involuntarily. "Many of us were pretty much forced to accept the 'take-it-or-leave-it' offer." she explained. "I'm getting a check every month, but I can't imagine sitting around doing nothing. And I really miss the interaction with people during the day. So I've been trying to start a consulting business, primarily targeted at the travel industry."

"How about you, Bob?" Even though it was his turn, I had asked Bob to do something unnatural—to share personal information about himself. "I work as a software designer for eData Systems," he said, in a soft, measured voice.

"Aha!" I thought to myself. "I had this fellow pegged!"

"Are you married? Do you have kids?" Sue had taken over the role of inquisitor.

"I'm not married. My friend Sarah and I live together. We'll probably get married one day. Our 'child' is a golden retriever. We both work such crazy hours, there's no room in our schedule for kids."

"How about you, Frank?" Sue enquired.

"Well as I said before, my name is Frank Devlyn. I'm from Mexico."

"Devlyn? That doesn't sound Mexican," Sue interrupted.

"My dad was American of Irish descent, my mom is Mexican. I grew up with my feet in both countries, literally. We lived in Juarez, Mexico, but I went to school in El Paso, Texas. I have been bilingual for as long as I could talk. Gloria Rita and I have been married for 35 years and we have three daughters—all married now—and five wonderful grandchildren. My career has been spent in the family business. We operate a chain of optical stores across Mexico and now in several other Latin American countries."

"So what brings you here?" This time it was Bob who asked the question.

"Rotary. I'm serving as president of Rotary International this year and am supposed to speak at a big event tonight honoring some of our major supporters of The Rotary Foundation."

"Rotary?" said Bob, with a puzzled look. "What's Rotary?"

But before I had a chance to answer, the cab driver startled us all by announcing we had arrived at the station. We had been so engrossed in conversation that we had not even noticed the fog had thinned to a light mist. I paid the cab driver, and having learned we were destined for the same train, the three of us walked together to the ticket office. Five minutes later we found our platform, where the train was waiting.

I think we already sensed a certain kinship that comes from people who are thrown together in times of adversity. An hour earlier I was frustrated at having my well-planned schedule disrupted. Then chance put me alongside two really nice people—I won't call them strangers because I believe strangers are only friends we have yet to meet.

The conductor told us the journey would take three and a half hours. As we boarded the train, we knew we need not ask whether we should sit together. We walked through the corridor searching for an empty compartment as the train lurched forward; none of them had three empty seats. Finally, near the back of the train, there was a compartment with just one man among the six seats. "Looks like this is it," said Sue.

"So!" I said. "You asked me, 'What is Rotary?' Before I answer, let me turn the question around. Bob, what do **you** think Rotary is?"

Bob reflected for several seconds, rubbing his right hand across the light stubble he was cultivating on his chin. "Isn't it, like, the Chamber of Commerce or something? Is the Rotary the same as Lions? I think my girlfriend's father is in Rotary. I've heard of the Rotary club, and I remember seeing their signs outside hotels and on the highway, but I have no real idea what it is or what it does."

"Sue, what do you think a Rotary club is?"

"While I was in high school, I won an essay contest. It was on how we should each do our part to help society, and it was sponsored by Rotary. Consequently, I had to read my essay at the local Rotary club to receive the prize. I was terrified of speaking to a group back then—of course, now, you can't shut me up," she said with a laugh. "Anyway, I practiced my talk over and over again, and on the big day I remember a bunch of old men all wearing name badges. It was a *Who's Who* of our town. The bank manager, the mayor, Mr. Schmidt of Schmidt's Supermarkets was there. So was Father Emil of St. Mary's Church, the police chief...like I said, there were a lot of influential people there. But what I've never forgotten is that halfway through my speech, I heard the sound of snoring. I looked up, and there was one of the members, sound asleep. That was over 30 years ago, but when I think of Rotary, I still think of an old boy's club—and the guy who slept through my speech."

I suddenly became aware of the man whose solitude we had interrupted. Far from seeming upset at our occupation of his previously-private compartment, he seemed genuinely interested in what Sue was saying. Our eyes met.

"Hi! I'm Frank Devlyn," I said offering my hand across the aisle.

"Duncan Thorpe," he said, as he grasped my hand in a firm, vigorous shake. He was an older man, maybe 65 or 66; tall, thin, and with a body that looked like the reward for years of regular exercise and healthy eating. I filled him in on who we were and how we came to be riding the train together.

"You can keep your jet planes," said Duncan, with a dismissive wave. "I spend 43 years in the rat race, running for planes, hoping for upgrades, worrying about how delays would mess up my meeting plans. I used to wonder what it was like to ride the rails. Now I ride the trains by choice. I retired last year from DuPro Chemical Company. My second wife passed away six years ago and I love to travel, to experience life and this beautiful country. So I buy a senior citizen rail pass and go where **I** want to go, **when** I want to go there. I've finally found out how to make the journey as interesting as the destination—just as with life itself.

"Ah, a philosopher, too, eh?" I said, with a smile.

"So how would you describe Rotary, Frank," asked Bob, his left-brain personality bringing the conversation back to where it had been heading before we met Duncan.

"You know, if somebody wanted to describe Sue's former employer, South American Airways, you might get different answers. One might say, 'I'm a proud citizen, and this is my national airline. They understand my language and culture.' Another might answer, 'It's got the best service in the air,' and others, 'South American Airways has the best fares,' or, 'South American Airways' pilots are the safest,' or, 'I fly them because their flight attendants are fabulous.' All of these people would be right. They have different perceptions of South

American Airways, depending on their personal experiences with the company.

"Rotary is the same. It began almost 100 years ago, in 1905, when a young lawyer moved to Chicago to establish his practice. It was a dog-eat-dog business environment back then and he yearned for the friendly, trustworthy way of life he had witnessed in the tiny Vermont village of his upbringing. So he started a club where business and professional people could become friends. It soon became an oasis of companionship in a desert of corruption and greed.

"It was the first of what some would today call networking clubs. Who wouldn't want to buy a suit from the tailor who had befriended you? And of course, if you were that tailor, you would buy your coal from the coal merchant in your Rotary club, and so on. They didn't *have* to trade with one another, they *wanted* to. Pretty soon, other people in the community wanted to do business with those merchants who promised fair and ethical treatment for all, and the Rotary Code of Ethics was adopted by dozens of trade associations across the United States and in many other countries. That's what we call Vocational Service. Rotarians act as ethical lighthouses, bright beams of integrity that are seen throughout their community and around the world.

"Rotarians have for almost 100 years cared deeply about their communities. It was Rotary that launched the crippled children's work which today is known as the Easter Seals Society. There are more than 30,000 Rotary clubs in large cities and small villages around the globe, and in every one of them the club is building parks, caring for the needy, working with kids, and undertaking tens of thousands of projects every year to make those towns a better place to live and work. That is our outreach we call Community Service.

"But you know, I should also mention that in addition to all those Rotary clubs, we have auxiliaries, typically made up of spouses and family members of Rotarians that undertake millions of hours of volunteer service on countless projects in their local communities as well as for international projects. Then we have 6,650 Interact clubs in 130 countries—that's like Rotary in high schools, and Rotaract, comprised of young adults, has 6,500 clubs in 146 countries with another 150,000 members. And in some countries local Rotary clubs sponsor Rotary Community Corps groups that also do invaluable local community service work.

"International Service has been a focus of Rotary since the early 1920s. It was Rotary that was the driving force to establish UNESCO. Rotarians were invited to participate in the founding of the United Nations. Rotarians in South America accomplished what governments could not: they literally brought together warring sides in a bitter border conflict between two countries and worked out a peace arrangement. Today, the jewel in our crown is what we call PolioPlus: Rotary's gift to the world for our 100th anniversary in 2005. We have immunized two *billion* children against polio since 1988 and have reduced the number of polio cases by more than 90 percent. We have eliminated polio completely in the Western Hemisphere, Europe, Western Pacific and China. By 2005, we will have wiped the disease off the face of the earth. And because Rotary has no political or religious ties, many countries in the midst of civil war have declared 'Days of Tranquility,' during which we went in and immunized every single child.

"Sue, you mentioned receiving a prize from a local Rotary club when you were a student. That barely scratched the surface of what Rotary does to help young people's education. A Rotary Foundation scholarship is worth about $25,000 and we award roughly 1,200 of them every year. In my year as president of Rotary International, we've spent more than $25 million in educational scholarships—and that's just the tip of the iceberg.

"But Rotary starts in the local club. And we emphasize Club Service so that the original intent of good fellowship, fun, camaraderie, and friendship is still accomplished. Personally, I had lots of friends before I joined my local Rotary club in 1970, but the best friends I've ever had have come as a result of my Rotary membership.

"So Bob, we're not a Chamber of Commerce, *per se*. But we are a group of business and professional leaders who can make things happen in our communities—both local and far away. And Sue, you'll be happy to know we stopped being an 'Old Boy's Club' many years ago. There are many women members—even club presidents and district governors—nowadays. And I doubt anybody will fall asleep when you address the Rotary club meeting now."

"I had no idea the Rotary club did all that," Bob admitted. "It's as if Rotary clubs and Rotarians are the community's best-kept secret."

"It's true that in the past many Rotarians and their clubs preferred to do their service work quietly. They didn't want to blow their horns," I explained. "But that is changing. We've got a great story to tell and we're proud to tell it. We know that there are a lot of people out there who would make wonderful Rotarians if they only knew what the organization does. Speaking of which, would **you** be interested in joining Rotary?"

There was a palpable change on their faces.

"I had the chance once," Duncan replied. "I'm retired, so I guess I've missed the opportunity."

"I'd love to, but there's no way I could. Not right now," Sue declared.

"Me neither. No way," said Bob.

I remember thinking, in that flash that takes all of a split second to reach the brain: "How could these people not be jumping at the opportunity? Rotary would change their lives for the better, and they would be wonderful additions to the clubs in their communities. I wonder what I have to do to get them beyond saying 'That's nice,' to making them enthusiastic about joining."

And so I decided to come right out and ask them.

"Why do you say that?"

My most memorable Rotary experience happened the first week in January 1992. My Rotary Club of Shrewsbury was one of 6 Rotary Clubs that started and sponsored the first Rotary Club in Kiev, Ukraine. The clubs involved were from Vancouver, B.C; Edinburgh, Scotland; Toronto, Canada; Washington, Michigan, and Shrewsbury, Ma. USA. One member from each club met every six months for two years. Each club representative agreed to visit Kiev on a six month rotating basis. My turn was set for the first week of January 1992. A Rotary meeting of the Provisional Kiev Club was set for Tuesday. My arrival on Sunday was complicated by a message that "Tuesday meeting was cancelled." A meeting was held the following Saturday with 65 enthusiastic new Rotarians. Why Memorable? I was a visiting Rotarian to a country of 52 million that just declared Independence from the USSR. Introduction of the first Rotary Club in over 70 years, and the Tuesday meeting was cancelled because, for the first time in over 70 years the Orthodox Christmas was declared a National Holiday.

—Arthur R. Dobson
Past Club President
Rotary Club of Shrewsbury
Shrewsbury, Ma. USA

Voluntary contributions to The Rotary Foundation, along with volunteer service time by Rotarians, built and operate this homeless shelter in Bangladesh.

A Rotary volunteer explains the importance of a balanced diet at this Rotary World Community Service nutrition project.

CHAPTER 2

WIIFM

"Look," said Duncan. "I don't want to seem selfish, but I've paid my dues. I don't need any lessons in ethics—I've never cheated anybody in my life. I've worked hard, paid my taxes, donated to charity. Now it's time to take care of myself first. I don't see any interest for me in Rotary."

Sometimes, I thought to myself, I can identify with how missionaries must feel when they know they have a great "product" but are confounded by people who are unwilling to open their minds to the message. "Duncan," I began, smiling as I wagged my finger at him. "I bet I know your favorite radio station. And Sue, Bob, even though we've all just met, I know your favorite radio station, too."

"*Radio* station? How in the world did we get on *that* subject?" asked Sue, with a puzzled look.

"Duncan just brought it up unwittingly," I replied. "You see, the call letters of your—and my—favorite radio station are WII-FM. And they stand for, 'What's In It For Me?'

"I know that whether I'm talking to my wife, my employees, my customers, or the volunteers in Rotary, the moment I ask them to do something, they subliminally ask themselves, 'What's in it for me?' If Devlyn Optical put out an advertisement that said, 'Buy your glasses here,' nobody would do so. But if we acted proactively and knew our customers were listening to WII-FM, then we could design an advertising campaign that touched on the benefits to them of shopping with us.

"Duncan just said he has paid his dues to society and quickly protested that he didn't want to seem selfish by not joining Rotary. He's not being selfish. He *has* worked hard all his life. And he has the right to tune in to WII-FM.

"What about you, Bob? When you ask the question, 'Why should I join Rotary?' how does the answer sound?"

"I'm as far away from Duncan's reasoning as you can get," said Bob. "The e-commerce business is unbelievably competitive. Duncan stayed with one company for 40 years; in our industry, you get a 'long service' pin for staying with the firm 12 months. The term 'dog eat dog' describes our industry on a good day; the pressure to perform is intense. We all work incredibly long hours, are always looking forward to break through new frontiers in technology, and always looking over our shoulders at younger guys who can move faster, better, smarter—and for less compensation—than us."

"To me, you *are* the young guys," Duncan interjected. "You mean you are worried about the younger generation, too?"

"I'm 31 and I'm the old man in my department. We have a dozen brilliant young people in their mid- to late twenties who are aggressive; they want it all and they want it now. One of our challenges is the growing number of small start-up companies that have a low cost structure, a rapid response time and a real entrepreneurial spirit.

"I admit, I make a lot of money. I earn a bonus of as much as 150% of my salary each year—but that adds to the pressure on me because it's all tied in to meeting certain performance standards. It would take me about this long ..." he snapped his fingers in the air "... to decide whether I would risk this month's bonus so I could go to lunch with a bunch of Rotarians with whom I have nothing in common."

I took a deep breath. "So what you are both saying—and my guess is that Sue is thinking this also—is, 'What's in it for me to spend an hour or 90 minutes at a Rotary club meeting?' Is that right?"

"Well, yes. I'm not *opposed* to what you guys do. I just don't see how joining Rotary would benefit me," Sue answered. Her response drew concurring nods from Duncan and Bob.

"Since you spoke up, let me start with you then," I began, looking at her. "You are starting your own consulting business, Sue. Who will your clients be?"

She thought for a moment before answering, as if to prepare a concise definition of her target audience. "I will focus on three types of client," she summarized. "I will work with travel agents to help them design business plans that take advantage of the changing ways their customers will buy travel in the future. Travel agents literally need to reinvent themselves, and I can help them do that. My second client category is the corporate travel account. After 25 years in the airline industry, I know that business inside out, and I can show companies how to save a great deal of money on their travel costs. Finally, I will consult with groups on how they can negotiate for lower tour costs, reduce their stress, and design a better package."

"And how do you find those clients?" I asked.

"That's the big question, isn't it?" she replied. "It's my biggest problem. I'm just starting out and I can't afford to advertise. I was thinking of printing a brochure and buying a direct-mail list, and getting a Website, but everybody already gets so much print and electronic junk mail, I worry that my little piece would get ignored. I'd have to say that my best opportunities are through personal contacts."

"Sue, Rotary is the biggest networking club on earth. I attended a luncheon meeting at a club yesterday. It had about 60 members, and just the people at my table included a bank vice president, a lawyer, the CEO of the local hospital, an accountant, and the head of human resources for the gas company. Oh, and there was a promotions director from a newspaper and a funeral director, too. Do you think any of them work for organizations that book business travel?"

"Of course!" she exclaimed. "Especially the bank, the gas company, and the newspaper."

"Now let's turn on your favorite radio station. What would be in it for you to have developed a good, friendly, trusting relationship with those executives? If you had . . ." but I was not able to finish my sentence.

"Relationships are *everything* in my business," she interrupted. "If we had the kind of friendship you described, and if I told them I'd like to make a presentation to their decision makers on how I could save them a lot of money, I'd have to believe I'd get a fair hearing."

"The fact is, when Rotary began, back in 1905, the original intent was for people from different businesses and professions to network together. It soon became a group of people who shared the same commitment to high ethics and trustworthiness, and given the choice of helping one another or giving business to total strangers, Rotarians preferred to patronize other Rotarians. To a great extent that's still true. Now don't misunderstand me: Rotary is not a reciprocal trading club, and you should not join Rotary *expecting* business from other members with profit as your motive. But many of the best Rotarians in the organization's 96-year history first joined Rotary because they thought it would help their business.

"I remember vividly as a new Rotarian in 1971, attending the international convention of the Federation of World Optometric Associations in Amsterdam. I was the past president of the Optometric Association of Mexico and they had entrusted me to obtain recognition of our organization from the world body. That morning I had been told how slow the process would be—there was a lot of red tape ahead of me. At lunchtime I made up at the Amsterdam Rotary Club—in fact, it was my first visit to a Rotary club outside of my immediate home area. There at my table sat the leaders of six of the world optometric associations—and simply because I was a fellow Rotarian, they treated me as if I was their peer. I was thousands of miles from home and didn't know a soul, yet those people helped me speed through our application in record time, simply because of our common bond of Rotary. Wearing that little Rotary pin has been beneficial on so many occasions, and Rotarians from other professions have often told me the same thing.

"Another case I'll never forget is when 30 years ago as a young entrepreneur I had a booth at a trade show that catered to ophthalmologists. My goal was to find new customers for our company, and it so happens that while I was working our exhibit one day a distinguished ophthalmologist from Veracruz, Mexico, came up and poked at my chest repeatedly as he said, 'I'm going to do business with you because I know I can trust you,' I couldn't figure out why he kept poking at me. Then it dawned on me: he was tapping my Rotary pin. He was the first of many people who have told me they choose to do business with me because I am a Rotarian. At that same trade show, many other leading ophthalmologists identified themselves as Rotarians. That opened important doors to get to the leaders in my profession, because in my business as in most businesses, people follow the leaders."

I turned to Bob. "What do you want from life, Bob? Some people might say you've got it all: a great job, fabulous income, pretty girlfriend, the Porsche, the golden retriever..." I paused for dramatic effect and lowered my voice. "*Do* you have it all? What is missing in your life that you would still like to have?"

"Oh, man. This conversation is getting *way* too deep," Bob answered, just a little defensively. "I suppose what I want today is different from what I wanted when I was young."

"When you were young! You're only 31 now! You're at the beginning of your professional life," Duncan interjected.

"I know I'm young, but I feel differently about my goals today than I did even a couple of years ago," he continued. "What do I want? On the professional level, I would like to go into management. Then I could delegate some of the projects I get assigned now that keep me up, burning the midnight oil. The problem is, I don't have any leadership training; my only qualifications are my programming and computer proficiency. To get into higher management at eData Systems, you need technical skills *and* people skills. I wish I had the latter."

"What else?"

"I guess I also feel a little guilty about my level of income and my conspicuous consumption. There's a lot of peer pressure among my friends to drive the flashiest cars and own the latest gadgets—and that's fine, because I love gadgets and toys. But I've recently had to start going abroad to our facilities in India and the Philippines. Last year I also had to visit Peru. When I saw how some of the poor people lived in those places, it really troubled my conscience."

"It's not just in India that you'll find poor people," said Duncan. "We've got plenty of them right here at home."

"Yes, I know that," Bob rejoined. "But I've never seen crippled children squatting in sewage ditches here. I've never seen entire families rooting through garbage dumps looking for food scraps before. That really affected me. No human being should have to live like that."

"So what did you do about it?" asked Sue.

"We have a pretty good program at work called the 'We Care' campaign. The company matches our donations up to a certain limit and makes grants to charities. Last month, just after I got back from the Philippines, I donated my entire quarterly bonus check to the We Care campaign."

"How did that make you feel?" I enquired.

"Pretty good, I guess."

"You don't sound convincing."

"Well, I'm glad I did it, but, like, I wrote the check—and that was it. I didn't *see* it help. I didn't get much joy out of my contribution—not that I made it for *my* benefit, of course."

As Bob was trying to explain his feelings, I suddenly remembered reading an article recently that reported the results of a sociological study. It showed how, in Western cultures, there has been an attitude change between Bob's generation and that of his parents. Older people joined clubs and supported organizations. Generation X generally does not feel compelled to join clubs nor support institutions. As older donors—who willingly sat on the local hospital board, and made generous contributions to the alumni association and health research societies—die off, the younger generation prefers not to patronize institutions, but to support causes. Just as they live their lives, seeking immediate gratification and rewards, so they want to give to causes where they can see results quickly. That is why charity walkathons, volunteerism projects, Habitat for Humanity blitz builds, and short-term mission trips are very popular among young people, while giving to, say, cancer research or the college endowment fund is declining.

"Bob, first of all, we in Rotary need the people who write the checks, too, so whether or not you decide to become a Rotarian, don't stop contributing to worthy causes. I'm not going to try and sell you on Rotary just to hear my own voice, but I feel as if I've come to understand you, so will you permit me to share what's in my heart?" He looked genuinely interested in hearing what I had to say, and told me to go ahead.

"I believe you can help Rotary, and Rotary can help you—on both a personal and professional level. Let's start with your career. When you go to computer conferences, the only thing people talk about is computers, right?"

"Agreed. Those meetings are strictly for high-tech junkies. I don't even take Sarah, my girlfriend, because she says they are so boring," he explained.

"When you go to a Rotary club meeting, you will interact with leaders from a broad spectrum of businesses and professions. It is a valuable membership benefit to be able to mix, and become friends with, people with knowledge and influence beyond your own industry. And because Rotarians enjoy helping other Rotarians, the chances are they will ask you to share your expertise in computers. At the same time, you will have a rich reservoir of information available on subjects you are not yet familiar with."

"Such as?" he asked.

"When I bought my first home, I didn't know anything about the pitfalls of home buying and financing, so I asked two Rotarians who were experts in that field. When I have a question about investing, or which Caribbean island would make the perfect vacation spot—I can go to people in Rotary who are knowledgeable in those subjects and who I know will not deceive me or try to "hard sell" me.

"You mentioned wanting to go into management. Most companies, especially large firms, recognize the need to be perceived as good corporate citizens. They encourage their people to become involved in civic organizations; they know such an affiliation broadens the employee's personality. Let's say that eData Systems is considering you and one of your peers for advancement. They only have one opening and the two of you are equally qualified. If you were CEO of the company, which candidate do you think would be more rounded, more likely to be a good representative for eData: the other guy who is simply a software engineer, or you who is equally well qualified but who also shows commitment to the community and has a track record of accomplishments beyond the office?"

"I see your point," said Bob. "But do you really think that matters?"

"It sure did at DuPro Chemical," Duncan interjected. "When you got to a certain level, if you weren't involved in civic activities, you were *told* to be."

"Here's another benefit: The chances are, the club you join will invite you to work on a committee in the service area of your greatest interest. Let's just say for a moment that you love kids and you volunteer to serve on the committee that evaluates essays for a club scholarship contest."

"Like the one I won!" exclaimed Sue.

"You will learn many of the traits that you will need in your managerial role, such as planning, people skills, motivation, how to persuade people of differing personalities and opinions to follow your lead. Even as a young guy—younger than you are—and long before I joined the Rotary club, I remember reading a book in the "Self Help" section of a bookstore. It talked about the importance of networking and said one of the best ways to do that was to join a service club—and Rotary, it advised, was the best of them all.

"If you join your local club and chose to progress, perhaps to a club officer, club president, even district governor or Rotary International president, you will learn leadership skills that you can use in your work for the rest of your life. Look at me, I used to be terrified of public speaking, and now, there's never a city that I speak in where people don't come up afterwards and tell me how I've inspired them. Rotary did that for me. Can you see how that helps me when I have to inspire my people back at Devlyn Optical to reach the next level? Can you see how those skills would benefit you in your career?"

"Well, sure," he agreed.

"One final thing, Bob. I know several fast-track guys like you, and they tell me that because they work such crazy hours, most of their friends tend to be their coworkers. Is that true in your experience?"

"It's funny you should bring that up," he said. "Last night, Sarah and I had an argument because she doesn't want to go to the cookout some friends are having on Saturday. She said they are not *our* friends, they're *my* friends, and everyone else at the party will be from eData, with whom she has nothing in common."

"I remember the words of Ralph Waldo Emerson," I said, quickly trying to recall the exact quotation. "'He who has a thousand friends has not a friend to spare.' We *need* friends for our own physical and mental well being. And yet when those friends' only link is through our work, we risk being unable to move from the stress of work to the joys of friendship alone, because it's likely our conversation will constantly revert back to work matters. I'm not saying we should give up those work friends; I'm saying we need friends from other sources, too. We need a balance.

"Our world is becoming increasingly impersonal and technology driven. Where we used to chat with the local shopkeeper and take long walks in the woods, now we buy over the Internet and dash off a quick e-mail to friends. We sit behind computer screens all day at work and come home to computer or TV screens all evening. We are becoming increasingly disconnected from that which we should hold the most precious: family, friends, and our community. What kind of life is that?

"I cannot begin to tell you how many friends I have made through Rotary. Sometimes, I get to a club meeting feeling really stressed because of work or travel, or one of life's other concerns. Then I walk in and share a few jokes, have fun, learn something new, feel myself growing—both as a person, and professionally—and have the real joy of being with friends. *That's* what's in it for me, Bob. And that's what's in it for you."

"I think it's good to mix with young people," Duncan volunteered. "It keeps me feeling useful. I had a young fellow teach me how to use the Internet recently. It was great! He showed me how to do so many things that I bought myself one of those laptop computers, and now I carry it on my trips. It's such fun to be able to search for information about a place that I'm visiting."

"That's wonderful," I agreed. "Now, Duncan, if *you* tuned in to WIIFM and I was the announcer, here's what I'd tell you: there's nothing lonelier than being in a strange town and not knowing a soul there. Can you imagine how different you'd feel in knowing that every single day of any week you'd be welcomed as the honored guest at 30,000 Rotary clubs in towns and villages across 199 countries? I cannot tell you how many times I've made up at a Rotary meeting and the local members have invited me home to dinner the next day, or taken me on a tour of their city.

"You see, folks, Rotary was started by Paul Harris, a lonely man who wanted to make friends in the big impersonal city. It began as a club to fill that most basic human need: the need for fellowship and belonging. It later evolved into an organization that gives us the opportunity to give back to our community and to needy people around the world. All of those opportunities still exist in Rotary. And they all satisfy the WIIFM question.

"For those who want to feel connected, Rotary helps give us a sense of community. For those wishing they could expand their business contacts, Rotary offers unbeatable networking opportunities. For those who are lonely, it is a wellspring of friendship and support. For those on the fast track, it provides tools and opportunities to help you become a better leader. For those who love to travel, it's like pulling into a strange town almost anywhere on earth and finding the welcome light illuminated on the front porch."

"I can see why they elected you president of Rotary International," said Sue, to the affirming nods of the other two.

"Thanks for the compliment," I said. "But you are giving credit to the wrong guy. I'm not the one who built Rotary to what it is today. I'm simply one of the messengers. If any of the other 1.2 million Rotarians had been sitting in this seat, he or she would have told you a similar story. Sue, you were with South American Airways for 25 years, Duncan, you stayed loyal to DuPro for 40 years. Even Bob travels the world promoting the attributes of his company. I'm the same way with Rotary, only in a voluntary capacity. You see, in order to be convincing, you've got to be convinced. And I'm convinced that membership in Rotary is one of the greatest honors that a person can be offered, and through that membership, Rotarians can make a real difference in their own lives, their communities, and the lives of others.

"You know, there might be an opening for someone in your line of business in the Rotary club in your town. Would you consider joining?"

I helped a patient to undergo cataract operation at Nellore Rotary Eye Hospital. The patient said, "I find God in the shape of Rotarians. I had no money even to have a normal check up with a doctor. But you Rotarians have given me total eye sight." He was in tears of joy. It was a moment of joy to me.

—Dodla Bharath Kumar Reddy
Past District Governor
Rotary Club of Nellore
Nellore, India

CHAPTER 3

Boring Old Men

It was Duncan who spoke first. He spoke with a clear strong voice and despite being retired, still addressed us with the same confident air that he must have used during his years as a manager with DuPro, one of the world's leading chemical companies.

"Several years ago—I was department manager at the time—I remember our community relations department urging us to join civic organizations. In fact, our plant manager was a Rotarian. He went on to become, I don't know what you call it, the head of a bunch of Rotary clubs."

"District governor?" I enquired.

"Yes, that title sounds familiar. From time to time he'd recruit me to go talk to high school students about career choices and business ethics. I know he was very active in Rotary right up to his death a couple of years ago."

Sue's eyes darted about as if she wanted to speak, but hesitated to do so. "Sue, what makes you so uncomfortable about joining Rotary?" She shot a glance at me, then at Bob, as if seeking his support; then the words came tumbling out.

"Well, hmmm, please don't take this personally, Frank. But I think of the Rotary club as a bunch of boring old men. During my career with South American Airways, I was sometimes asked to give programs on Brazil, or on the airline industry, to Rotary clubs. I know I'm still prejudiced by that incident when the guy slept through my essay recital, but honestly, Frank, the average age of some of these Rotarians is *dead*! My most enduring memories of those Rotary club visits are of consistently awful food and the feeling of being an intruder at the Old Boy's Club—with the emphasis on the *Old*."

"Did you ever go to a Rotary club meeting, Bob?" I asked, hoping for an uplifting response.

He brushed back the locks of hair that had fallen across his eyebrows and considered his words carefully before speaking. "No, I have never been invited to a Rotary club. And even if I were asked to join, I don't think I'd be interested."

"You said, 'No way!' when I asked you the first time. What made you say that?"

"Well, . . ." His voice trailed off. He looked out the window at what had become a bucolic scene of sheep grazing in lush green meadows. Graceful willow trees bordered a meandering stream, and as we raced past it all, a hawk swooped at lightning speed toward its unsuspecting prey.

" . . . the thing is, I've got nothing in common with a bunch of boring old men, as Sue calls them. I mean, you guys deserve a lot of credit for all the good work you do—those projects and programs you talked about earlier. But I would feel out of place in an old men's club. I like action. I don't want to sit around and reminisce about the good old days. Whether it's a project at work or a personal issue—such as a vacation—I like to dive in, figure out what needs to be done, and then do it. I'd be bored to death in what Sue calls The Old Boys Club."

It hurt me to hear these honest appraisals. But I had to admit; I had shared similar perceptions of Rotary the first time I was invited to a club meeting. I decided to share that experience with my traveling companions.

"You know, I was even younger than you when I joined Rotary, but I had the very same concerns," I said. Bob looked surprised.

"Don't look so shocked, Bob. I *was* young once, you know." Sue and Duncan laughed with him. "In fact, I bet we have a lot in common, even though we are separated by age, nationality, profession, and probably by religion and personal interests. I came out of college and wanted to make money, be a success in business, learn as much as I could about my trade, and have fun—not necessarily in that order."

"That's me!" he said, with a broad smile.

"That's *still* me," said Sue.

"That's *all* of us," added Duncan. "Even though I no longer go to an office every day, I still want to be good at what I do. I need to make money, mainly from my investment portfolio, but also from a little technical writing I do. And the whole reason I'm on this train journey is to have fun."

"My point exactly," I agreed. "You see, we—the four of us—have far more that unites us than what separates us."

"But you said Rotary was a club for boring old men," argued Sue.

"Hey, watch it young lady," interjected Duncan, wagging his index finger at her.

"No, I said my *perception* of Rotarians was that way," I explained. "Right out of college, my brother Jesse and I continued working in the family optical business in Mexico. One day we went on a business trip to Sulphur Springs, Texas, near Dallas. That was the headquarters of Southern Optical Supply Company, and its owners, Dr. James L. Crawford and his twin brother, Dr. John F. Crawford, were friends of our family.

"While we were there, Dr. James invited us to attend his Rotary club meeting. 'It would be good for you two young guys to meet people in the Rotary club,' he told us. Dr. John, who was a member of the Kiwanis club, took pleasure in telling us, 'Rotary is an old man's club!' But Jesse and I had already accepted Dr. James's offer, so off we all went. I saw things that day that I'll never forget. First, they weren't all old men. And second, regardless of age, they acted like boys again. They had fun with each other. They joked and kidded and there was a sense of true friendship and fellowship in the room. I remember being floored when they all called Dr. James Crawford—a man of great prestige and influence—'Hey, Jimmy!' And when Dr. Crawford introduced Jesse and me, although we were young, strangers, and from Mexico, they were hospitable and congenial.

"I still remember the speaker that day. He gave a presentation on insurance fraud. If I'd seen that subject listed at a conference I would have thought it sounded boring too. But it was fascinating. I learned things during that 20-minute presentation that have benefited me ever since.

"Jesse and I were impressed with Rotary but because of our age, it was almost 10 years before we were invited to join local Rotary clubs in our town. That was in 1970, and in the hundreds of club meetings that I've attended around the world ever since, I have always learned something that would benefit me either personally or professionally."

"OK, so maybe Rotary is not boring, but it's still an old man's club. That's why I don't see it as having any interest to me," said Sue.

"Hey! I warned you before about making comments about old men!" Duncan feigned such a protest that we all erupted in laughter.

"I can't win here, can I?" Sue replied. "OK, Duncan, I didn't mean to offend you. Besides, I don't think age is measured in years; it's measured in outlook, in attitudes, in personality. You see, I don't even think of you as 'elderly' or even as 'retired.' In just the time we've spent together today, I think of you as 'one of us.' Just as I don't *feel* like someone old enough to be Bob's mother, neither do I see you as being 'old.'" She reached over and grasped his hand. "Forgiven?"

"Sue, do you hear what you've just said?" I asked. "You have exactly corroborated my point about Rotary. It is a club where barriers disappear. The little compartments that society uses to *separate* people, even to discriminate against folks who are different from themselves, vanish at the doors to the Rotary club. You just said that you don't put Duncan in the category, 'old,' or see Bob as a 'young kid,' or me as 'the Mexican.' You see all of us as nice people, friends, perhaps, interesting fellow passengers on your journey.

"That's exactly how it is in Rotary. I meet thousands of Rotarians every year. It comes almost as a surprise to me when I realize the person I've been talking to is black, and that one is Hindu, the other fellow is a millionaire, this one's a world-renowned surgeon, and this person here is retired and on a fixed income. When we meet in Rotary, they all are simply "Sue," "Raul," "David," or "Mary." And to continue your own analogy but with a philosophical slant, I suppose Rotarians come together to share a journey: we are all on the journey of life, and we share the common desire to serve humankind so others less fortunate can also enjoy that journey."

"Frank, I've been in sales all my life, and you're quite a salesman," said Sue. "But even if you've won me over with the fact that Rotary is not a club for *Boring* or *Old* men, it's still a *men's* organization."

Before I had time to answer her, the refreshments trolley came around. Duncan and I ordered coffee, Bob had a Coke, Sue asked for a Diet Coke. I turned to Sue.

"I hate to seem argumentative, but nothing could be further from the truth. Sure, Rotary began as an all-male organization, but remember, in those days, very few women held managerial roles or owned businesses. They weren't even allowed to vote. By the seventies, there was a growing movement to allow women into Rotary, and I was one who fought for that change. It wasn't fair to leave women out of the loop when movers and shakers met to discuss things of importance. My own mother is a doctor of optometry who, at the age of 82, still comes to work every day. She was honored as Woman of the Year by the business and professional women's organization of Juarez, Mexico—a city of 1.5 million people; yet she was not entitled to join Rotary, and that really bothered me. Rotary International removed all gender-specific references from its membership criteria back in 1987. There are tens of thousands of women Rotarians today, including many who are club presidents and district governors. There are even some clubs where the majority of Rotarians—or even the entire membership—is female. And once again, when we meet at conferences or during inter-club visits, we don't see that person as a *woman* Rotarian, but simply as a *fellow* Rotarian. I must say, Sue, that when we fought for women to be admitted into Rotary, it was women like you we had in mind."

"Gee, when this conversation began and these two kept talking about boring old men, I was thinking of changing seats," said Duncan with a deadpan expression. "Frank, I think your explanation was downright interesting. I feel like my dignity has been restored, like I've won the argument—and I'm not even a Rotarian!"

"Why aren't you?" I asked.

Joining a Rotary Club has added a whole new dimension to my life. We are all extremely busy with our families and businesses and have no time for helping others and meeting new friends. Rotary has changed all that for me. By spending a few hours in service to my club I have enhanced my circle of friends locally, regionally, and internationally. Rotary has also raised my self-worth by allowing me to contribute to others in need locally and internationally and I truly feel that my presence on this earth can make a small difference in the happiness of others. My husband and I are both Rotarians in different clubs and we feel that no matter where we travel there will be a hand of friendship extended to us by our fellow Rotarians anywhere in the world. Join a Rotary Club so you can enjoy the pleasure of enriching your world.

—Emma Sue Smallwood
Club President
Rotary Club of Hinsdale
Hinsdale, Illinois USA

Another new member joins Rotary.

Interact is Rotary's club for high school teenagers. Here an Interact club in Brazil cooperates with their sponsoring Rotary club on a community service project.

CHAPTER 4

Busy, Busy, Busy

As if to give Duncan a few moments to reflect on my question, the train entered a tunnel. For almost a minute we hurtled through the darkness, like a rocket ship through space, except for the noise, which made conversation impossible. Then just as quickly, we were outside again, the brilliant sunshine causing Duncan and Sue, who were seated beside the window, to squint.

"I don't have time to join Rotary. I'm too busy," Duncan declared.

"But I thought you'd retired," argued Bob.

"Being retired doesn't mean sitting in a rocking chair at the nursing home, waiting for the undertaker," Duncan shot back. Now it was Bob's turn to look sheepish. "Sorry, Bob. I didn't mean to snap at you. The fact is, I kind of wish I had joined a group like Rotary when I was employed at DuPro Chemical Company. They do a lot of good in the community, and my father always taught me that the best way to pay back our Creator for the blessings He gave me was to help others who haven't been as fortunate. But Rotary makes you go to their luncheons every week, and when I was with DuPro, I had so many meetings and business trips; I could never have kept up with the attendance requirements.

"Now I'm retired. But I volunteer to tutor some at-risk kids in chemistry and math at an after-school program, and once a week I read books and magazines to the blind at a nursing home. Plus I love to travel. Always have. I'm single; my kids are all grown and live far away now. I promised myself that once I retired I would see more of this great country and the world beyond it—at a more leisurely pace, so I try to take about one week a month to travel. Having to attend a Rotary club meeting every week would tie me down."

"You mean joining Rotary requires going to the meeting *every single week?*" asked Bob, seeming aghast at such a proposition.

"Yes, that's my understanding," said Duncan. "I remember asking about it back when DuPro encouraged its managers to join service clubs. The guy I spoke to said that I'd have to be at every meeting, and that if I missed . . . I think it was two or three meetings . . . I'd be thrown out of the club."

"Wow! They don't even do that at church. And God makes the rules there!" chirped in Sue.

I suddenly became aware of three sets of eyes interrogating me as if I were the person responsible for making such unreasonable demands on their time. This was a tricky topic to handle. Rotary does have attendance requirements, but they are often misunderstood and exaggerated. Most modern Rotary clubs will go out of their way to accommodate a busy member's schedule and are flexible in their attitudes toward attendance.

"The fact is, Rotary has never had a rule that requires members to attend every meeting," I began. "Nor have they had one that said 'Miss three and you're out.' The official rules say that you should make 60 percent of your home club's meetings, but the key here is to communicate. Be proactive and let your club leaders know that you travel a lot or will have trouble making some meetings.

"In the past, certain clubs were quite strict in their interpretation of attendance rules. Those rules often called for membership to be forfeited if a Rotarian missed four consecutive club meetings. But today, most clubs are much more flexible. They recognize that the old nine-to-five workday doesn't exist for most of us. Many families have two working parents and their kids are more active in sports and other extracurricular activities. Rotary clubs want good members, and good members are usually busy members. Remember, the chances are, the people on the club's board have the same demands on their time as you."

"You said, 'Nine to Five.' That's beyond my comprehension for a workday," said Bob, shaking his head in disbelief. "In my firm, most people never leave the office until six-thirty or seven in the evening, and I'm usually there until at least eight o'clock. My girlfriend is already complaining about the hours I work. I can't imagine what she'd say if I told her that I'm not coming home for dinner tonight because I'm going to the Rotary club."

"Bob, the last thing you young folks want is unsolicited advice from an old geezer like me. But do you mind if I add something to what you just said?" asked Duncan.

"Sure. Go ahead."

"Thirty-five years ago, I was right where you are now. When you just spoke, I immediately felt a sense of *deja vu*. When I was your age . . ." He stopped, his eyes twinkling, ". . . well, first of all, I hated old guys starting sentences with, 'When I was your age . . .'"

Bob laughed aloud. "Go ahead. I've already learned things from you today. You have my permission to offer your advice."

"When I was in my twenties and thirties, I was a dynamo that never stopped. I thought my life's goals should be more money, promotions, and pleasing the company. I set my eyes on climbing that corporate ladder and nothing got in my way. When they threw new responsibilities at me, I was thrilled to accept them. I was what we today call a workaholic: first into the office and last to leave. And do you know what? I got the promotions. I earned the bonuses and the stock options. But let me tell you what I lost." Duncan's voice faltered. His eyes moistened noticeably.

"My family," he said, in a whisper.

"One Sunday as I was packing to go on yet another week-long business trip, my wife told me she was leaving me. She said she had watched me leave week after week, that I was better known to some hotel staff than to my own family. Nothing I could say would change her mind. I couldn't even cancel my trip because it was for a critical presentation I had to make to the executive board of DuPro, one that would influence my promotion to vice president. When I got home on Friday, she and the kids had moved out. Just a few weeks ago, my middle son—who's now 38 years old—made some very hurtful comments to me about how I was never there for his football games or for his sister's piano recitals.

"And you know the real kicker? When DuPro considered me for promotion to vice president later that year, they passed me over because the pending divorce indicated what they called 'an unstable personal life.' My dedication to the job cost me both my family and my career advancement.

"So Bob, you do whatever you need to do to be good at your job. But you have to make room in your life for something *beyond* work. I don't know much about Rotary, but if you don't want to do that, take an evening once a week to teach computer skills at the orphanage, or feed the homeless, or volunteer at the AIDS hospice, or take up painting. Don't tell me you don't have time. You *have* time. It's just a question of how *you* decide to spend that time. Do you spend every hour on yourself, or can you give an hour a week to someone who needs you?"

The train compartment fell silent for two or three minutes following Duncan's powerful personal testimony. I think we all felt great empathy for him, for now we saw his vulnerable side. He had worked hard all his life only to reach retirement as a man of professional accomplishment and personal loneliness. I wondered how people confuse those with whom they are friendly at work with friends. There is an enormous difference between work acquaintances and true friends, and we all need more of the latter.

"How long do Rotary club meetings last?" It was Sue who finally broke the silence, and I think we were all grateful to her for doing so.

"It depends on the club," I answered. "But generally, 60-90 minutes. There are many breakfast clubs whose meetings last only an hour. Some luncheon clubs go a little longer, and dinner club meetings normally go for an hour and a half. If you consider that you have to eat breakfast, lunch, or dinner somewhere anyway, attending a Rotary meeting involves a minimal extra amount of time—especially considering the benefits you get from it. And if you have an important commitment elsewhere, you can leave early.

"One of Rotary's most celebrated customs is what we call 'make ups.' In my case, my club meets on Tuesday evening at eight o'clock. Now let's suppose I cannot make my regular club meeting. Up to two weeks before that meeting date, or for two weeks after it, I can show up at any of the 30,000 Rotary clubs in 199 countries around the world—and count that toward my attendance back home.

"So Bob, let's say you join a lunch club—that way you can still be home with your girlfriend in the evening. On the day your club meets at noon, some work crisis occurs that requires your immediate attention. You might go to a nearby breakfast club a few days later for a makeup. Sue, you said you're traveling a lot to build up your consulting business. Whatever town you're visiting that is large enough for your potential clients who need a travel industry consultant, I guarantee there will be Rotary clubs that will welcome you. And Duncan, our rambling retiree over here, the same applies to you. You've got to eat *sometime*. Which is better, to sit alone for a meal, or to eat in the company of people who share your interests and whose very presence will brighten your day?"

"I hear what you're saying, Frank. But still, my greatest challenge is finding the time to do things," said Sue. "I'm retired—technically—and I'm busier now than I ever was at South American Airways. I joined a ladies golf league in the spring and we spend most of each Monday together. I've just started decorating the house from top to bottom, and my church has asked me to volunteer two days a week at their kindergarten. On top of all this, I want to get my consulting business up and running."

"Sue, I understand what you're saying and I think it's wonderful that you are doing these things. Let me ask you, why do you choose to spend every Monday with your golf group? Are you trying to improve your game so that you can play professionally? Do you make money at it?"

"Heavens, no!" she exclaimed, rolling her eyes skywards. "Far from it. Tiger Woods's career is safe from me. And as for making money, it costs me a small fortune by the time I've paid for my dues, the lunches—and all the balls I lose! The main reason I go is for the fun we have together. Some of those ladies are so hilarious. It's just a great day out."

"Aha!" I said. "So what you are saying is the camaraderie, the *fellowship* is so valuable to you that even though you've said you are a busy person, you *make* the time to attend, right? How about your church school volunteer work? How many members does your church have?"

"About six hundred."

"So if *you* couldn't spend two mornings there each week, chances are the school wouldn't fall to pieces?"

"No, of course not. It ran perfectly well without me for 30 years."

"So why give them eight hours of your precious time every week?"

"Because I want to, Frank. You can't imagine how good it makes me feel to help. My brother is a carpenter and volunteers to build houses for Habitat for Humanity. My best friend is a nurse practitioner who goes on medical missions to developing countries to share her expertise. I have no such skills. But when I can help a tiny child, I feel as if I'm having a positive influence on that person's whole future."

"OK, I understand," I assured her. "You *find* the time to volunteer because you feel so good after you've helped out. What I heard you say originally was that you had no time. But what you have really demonstrated is that you'll *find* the time if the right perceived benefits are there."

"Perceived benefits?" queried Duncan.

"Yes. All of you, at some level, think of Rotary—and your other life activities—as being mutually exclusive. It isn't. Let's take Rotary out of the discussion for a moment and talk about time in general. I'm no longer Frank Devlyn, president of Rotary International. Instead, I'm back in Mexico, running Devlyn Optical. We have a chain of 400 retail stores, plus several manufacturing plants in Mexico, and distributors spread across Latin America. Do you think I could fairly be described as a busy guy?"

"That sure meets my definition of the word, Frank," agreed Bob.

"On the face of it, there's no way I can manage the company, deal with the crises, plan for the future, spend time motivating my people—and all the thousands of other details and tasks that land on my desk. It comes down to time management. I separate every item on my 'To Do' list under three categories: A, B, or C. 'Must Do' items go on the A list, 'Should Do' items go on the B list, and 'Would Like To Do' tasks become C items.

"Life—and even business itself—is not just about making money or adding market share. What's the point of getting to the moment when you leave this earth with all the money you ever wanted, but having no friends, no family, and no inner satisfaction of having shared your blessings with those less fortunate? A priest once told me that in all the people he had ever heard share their last words, not one of them had ever expressed a wish at that moment for more money.

"So when I make my time management assignments, Rotary could be in any of the three categories. If it's participating in an important program—say, tutoring at-risk kids at the orphanage—that's a Must Do item for me. It gets scheduled in the same way as a serious business meeting. Going to my club meeting? That's usually a Should Do, and since we meet in the evening, it's rarely a problem for me. But if I have, say, an employee recognition dinner on a Tuesday evening, then that becomes my A item and I'll make up my missed meeting at another club two weeks before or after the meeting I miss.

"Is that any different to what the three of you already do? Bob, you seem to be married to your job, but if you spent the next two weeks in the hospital, would eData Systems go bankrupt?"

Bob smiled a wry smile. "I sometimes *think* I'm indispensable, but of course, the answer to your question is no, they'd get along fine without me."

"Exactly. So if they could survive without you for two weeks, don't you think they could manage if you spent an extra 30 minutes over lunchtime at a Rotary club meeting one day this week?

"Duncan," I said, turning my gaze to the man beside the window. "And Sue. If you *wanted* to go to a Rotary club meeting, you could find the time to do so, couldn't you? As intelligent, professional people, you would simply adjust your work and other activities to accommodate it. You might work faster, or more productively, or perhaps eliminate a time-wasting task. But just as you *found* time for golf or volunteering now, you'd find time for Rotary.

"If you miss a meeting here and there, it's no big deal. But think about this: every human being on earth is given precisely the same amount of time each day. We all get 86,400 seconds as the clock strikes midnight—and there's no carrying over allowed. How we spend that 86,400 seconds is up to us. There are 1.2 million Rotarians around the world, some retired, like Duncan; some computer gurus like Bob, some starting out their own business, like Sue here. Many of them have jobs with enormous time demands—surgeons, funeral directors, police chiefs, even optical people like me. But they all get 86,400 seconds every day, and having tried Rotary, they find it to be an easy and personally fulfilling choice to allot a few of those seconds to maintain their membership. Yes, they're busy. But haven't you ever heard the expression, 'If you want to get something done, ask a busy person to do it'? A great many Rotarians have told me that *because* they are so busy at work, the time they spend with friends at their Rotary meeting is like an oasis of sanity, they go back to work with their batteries recharged.

"I would like to make a final point. I don't want to 'sell' you on going to Rotary as a guilt trip or out of a sense of duty. Sue, you said that you play golf because you love the company of the other team members. Why is that?"

"Because we have fun together, and the other women in my golf group are such interesting people," said Sue.

"Duncan, I'll bet that when your turn to read to the blind people comes around, you can't wait to get there, right? Why is that?"

"I suppose in my case the answer is that I get a wonderful feeling from helping people who need help. I'm doing something that comes so easy to me yet which is beyond their grasp," said Duncan, thoughtfully. "They are always so nice, so grateful. The times I am scheduled to volunteer for them certainly become a priority in my schedule."

"There you go then," I agreed. "I don't go to Rotary with the same sense of obligation or dread that I have when I have a dental appointment. I go because I *want* to go. I know that I'll have fun, learn something new, meet some pretty neat people, help people in need, and I will always pick up something that will benefit me. Rotary isn't a tiresome obligation, it's the bright spot in my week. Many professional people are required to take continuing education every year to maintain their academic and technical proficiency. Rotary offers continuing education that sharpens our personal and practical skills.

"A Rotarian in Vienna told me recently, "I have had perfect attendance for nine years. But I don't go 100 percent of the time because I have to, I go because I *want* to. I thought about what he said when I was on an airplane later that day and realized that what he said goes directly back to WIIFM.

The value to him of going to that Rotary meeting is greater than the value of doing something else. In Mexico, I belong to a group called ACE, an association of chain-store owners. They have a meeting once a month, and for the 14 years that I've been a member I don't think I've ever missed a meeting when I am in town—not because I have to go, but because I know that at every single meeting there will be speakers and networking that will benefit me. I go because I *want* to go, just as you will find with Rotary."

"Frank, I showed up today for a 50-minute flight that I thought I would doze through," said Bob. "I never talk to people on planes, and I'd never even thought about alternatives to my lifestyle. At work and at home, 'I'm too busy' is just part of my vocabulary. In the last hour I've realized that perhaps I don't have the right priorities. I love my job. I love my girlfriend, my Porsche, my dog. But is that all I'm working so hard for? Maybe *busyness* has clouded my senses as to how I should be focusing my life."

It was a remarkably open admission from the young man who had not previously opened up and shared his personal feelings. Yet his admission rang true in all our hearts. We had too often fallen into the trap of becoming addicted to urgency. We knew we had all committed the crime of letting "being too busy" be the excuse—the barrier—that leads to do that which seems urgent rather than that which is important.

For several minutes, the train raced onward while silence reigned in our compartment.

My memorable experiences in Rotary are numerous. However, two come to mind immediately. The first being a visit to a hospital for Child Victims of Chernobyl in Kiev, Ukraine. We visited the hospital the first time in May of 1992 along with Rotary International President Saboo and a large delegation of Rotarians. We met many very sick children but I remember little Irena, a very sick girl who received a Barbie doll from my wife. When Irena was asked what we could bring her next year she said, "But this doll is everything I have ever dreamed of having, there is nothing more that you could bring for me." The following year we visited the hospital again only to find that little Irena had died just a few months earlier. The nurse said that Barbie had made Irena so happy in her last days and that she died with Barbie in her arms. Tears flowed from all of us as we looked at Barbie on the shelf.

—G.Ted Segodnia
Rotarian
Rotary Club of Coquitlam
Coquitlam, BC, Canada

CHAPTER 5

"Rotary Costs Too Much"

"**O**ne big concern I have about joining Rotary is the cost," admitted Sue. "I'm not earning as much as I was before South American Airways put me on early retirement. Besides, I'm spending quite a lot of money trying to develop my consulting practice. I don't see how I could afford the free-spending ways of a movers-and-shakers club."

"Good point," echoed Duncan. "I have to watch every cent I spend nowadays. What I've accumulated has to last me for the rest of my life. I don't get 150 percent bonuses like fast-track Bob over here."

"You know, I'm embarrassed to admit this, but I spend every month wondering how I'm going to pay my bills, too," said Bob. "I think one reason we haven't gotten married and had kids is that neither Sarah nor I are very good at managing our money. We earn a lot, but we've just developed a lifestyle where we spend everything we make. I never worried much about saving, first because I was young, second, because I have a ton of stock in my company. Then the stock market nose-dived last year and in little more than six months, my portfolio lost almost 80 percent of its value. I've talked to friends at work for advice, but they're all in the same boat—we all have pretty much our entire investment in high-tech companies such as eData. So there's no way I can afford to go throwing my money away on a Rotary club membership."

"Bob, the first thought that comes to mind is that you need Rotary now more than ever," I began. He looked startled at my statement. "I mean it. The first thing you're likely to find is a person who can give you professional advice on money management. Don't follow the crowd at work in jumping at hot tips and gut-feel investment notions. If the club you join doesn't have a money manager, ask for recommendations from other members whom you respect, such as a banker or accountant. Secondly, I know that a lot of these dot com companies that could do no wrong in recent years really got hit in the past few months. Suddenly, they don't seem to offer unbridled promises of fame and fortune to their employees. Many of them have gone out of business; others have cut back their employees. It seems to me that this is exactly the time when you should be broadening your horizons. Just in case something happens to your job, wouldn't it be comforting to have a network of a hundred or so influential business leaders with whom you have developed relationships of friendship and trust?"

"But that doesn't explain away the *cost* of membership," argued Duncan. What you said makes perfect sense for Bob to join, but it isn't going to help me any."

"But we were talking about cost," I reminded him. "And 'cost' is a relative term. I needed four sponsors *and* a $25,000 entrance fee to join the University Club. The Industrial Club charged my company $90,000 to get in plus annual dues. Membership in my golf club costs $120,000 to join, plus monthly dues of $650. There is no Rotary club on earth that charges that much—and no matter how prestigious the groups I just mentioned are, *none* of them have anything close to the world-wide prestige and influence of Rotary. And none of them do as much in a decade as Rotary does in a week for humankind.

"In Japan, Rotary membership is reserved for the highest echelon of business and professional leaders. It can easily cost $1,000 to get in and $5,000 a year to belong, especially in the main clubs of the big cities. That's extremely expensive by worldwide Rotary club standards, but is still a drop in the bucket compared to membership in a Japanese golf club. Now let me take you around the world. A friend of mine made up at a club in a tiny town in the mountains of North Carolina. He paid $4.50 for a nice lunch in a rustic cabin at the end of a dirt road and sat down with the farmers and small business owners who belonged to the club. "Wow! I can't believe you charge $4.50 for lunch," he said, making conversation with the Rotarian next to him—and marveling to himself at the fact that his home club charged $13. "I know, it's disgusting, isn't it?" the man responded, with a scowl. "The caterer just raised our meal price from $4. You think *you're* mad? Two guys quit the club over it." My three traveling companions laughed aloud.

"It's a true story. The point I'm reinforcing is that cost is relative. The cost of the weekly meal in that club is $4.50. In other clubs it's $12. In a very few high profile clubs in places like London, Paris, or Tokyo—it may be $35 to $50. But let me break down the cost of membership for you. Let's say the average monthly costs are $65. That includes your meal. Now what would you pay for dinner at a fairly nice restaurant anyway?" Including tax and gratuity?"

"Including tax and tip? I suppose around $13 or $14," said Duncan.

"Everyone agree with Duncan?" I asked, looking for consensus.

"The kind of places I go, I spend $14 on the *appetizer*," said Bob, more as a self-deprecating joke than a boast.

"And that's exactly why you have no money left over at the end of the month," Sue added.

"I feel like my mother is here," said Bob, looking around the compartment.

"Let's not fight," I chided playfully. "So we all agree that we've got to eat a meal anyway, and $14 is a reasonable cost. That's $56 of the $65 right there that goes to buying your meal four times a month. The other $9 is for your subscription to *The Rotarian* magazine and dues to the club, the district, and to Rotary International. Again, there are clubs with higher dues and some with lower, but $65 is about average. From time to time there are events that would cost more, such as conferences, special banquets, and the opportunity to contribute to The Rotary Foundation, but they are entirely optional."

"That sounds interesting," said Sue. "But my problem is that since the airline put me on early retirement, my income has shrunk while my household bills have stayed the same. I just don't have as much disposable income as I once had."

"I hear what you are saying, Sue. I really do. But I also heard you say that you spend quite a lot of money at a golf league every Monday. Now please don't think I'm arguing or saying you should give up the golfing group; my point is that you were in the same financial circumstances when you decided to join the women's Monday golf league and you *found* the money you need to play golf. And the reason you found that money is that you see golf with the ladies as being fun—it is worth the expense, in your eyes. Am I right?"

"Yes, I see what you are saying," she agreed. "When I found I was pregnant with our second daughter, we were worried about how we could afford another child. But when the blessed event occurred, we made adjustments; we never felt we were any poorer than we had been before she came along. I never thought I was contradicting myself, but now that I think of it, it costs me more to play golf in a week than you're saying it costs to belong to Rotary for a month."

"Now let's equate the price of membership with the benefits," I said, hoping that I didn't sound too much like a salesman going for the close. "Sue, which benefits of Rotary membership do you see as most beneficial to you?"

"Well, Frank, you've opened my eyes to several possibilities. Of course, there's the business networking opportunity. That really intrigues me because, as I said, I am convinced that the best way to develop my consulting business is through personal contacts. But it sounds as if members have fun at their club meetings. I *love* people—in case you couldn't tell—and it sounds as if Rotary would be a place to make new friends. My two daughters are both away at college and my husband Steve is a computer programmer who works late at the office most days—*like somebody else I know . . .*" she glared theatrically at Bob. "So I'm home alone a lot in the evening. That's so boring for me; I'd much rather be doing something useful."

"Is it worth $9 a month, plus the cost of your meal, for you to have so many of these benefits?" I asked. It was a rhetorical question. Everybody knew the answer.

"Bob, in your case, it's not so much a case of affording Rotary as it is of prioritizing the time and cost. When you tuned in to WIIFM a while ago, you heard several benefits that accrue through Rotary membership, some of which could have a life-long impact for you. If just one of them occurred, say, developing your leadership skills so that your company chose you for promotion, would that be worth $9 a month plus the cost of a breakfast once a week?"

"It would be more of an investment than a cost," he affirmed.

"Duncan, where are you planning to travel to on your next trip?"

"I leave at the end of the month for a two-week cruise through the Caribbean," he answered. "Because it's off season, I got a great senior citizen's rate. We'll visit Cancun, Cozumel, Jamaica, Puerto Rico, St. Thomas, Grenada, and Martinique."

My mind flashed back to an incident years ago when I was also on a Caribbean cruise. Wanting to maintain my perfect attendance record, I looked in the Rotary International directory for clubs that held their meetings at times when our ship was visiting their city. When we arrived in Fort-de-France, Martinique, I went to the club meeting just as it was about to begin. "Do you speak French?" the president enquired. I confessed that I did not. He then announced to his club members that the meeting would be conducted in English that day so the visiting Rotarian could understand everything. I told my traveling train companions this story, and others. Of simple acts of kindness showered on me all over the world—long before I became a Rotary International officer—simply because I walked into their club as a visiting Rotarian.

"In Florence, Italy, when I mentioned in passing that I wasn't particularly impressed with my hotel, the Rotarian I was sitting with insisted on picking me up the next morning and driving me to another hotel where the general manager, also a Rotarian, put me into a suite. In Geneva, Switzerland, I was enjoying the conversation with the Rotarian seated next to me. He drove my wife and me back to our hotel and even invited us to go sailing with him. When I asked his name, it was Phillipe Patek, grandson of the founder of the world-famous watch company, Patek Phillipe. In Vienna, Austria, a Rotarian I met at the local Rotary club absolutely insisted on taking me on a wonderful tour of his city that lasted until midnight.

"Do you see the benefit of being a part of that? How wonderful it is to be able to drop in on a group of like-minded people wherever your travels take you. In my business, I'm used to rationalizing the cost of everything we do. But after more than 30 years in Rotary, I can honestly tell you, you will never be able to balance the rewards you receive with the pittance that Rotary club membership costs you. You will remember the benefits of membership long after you have forgotten what that membership cost."

My wife Karolina and I were privileged to be part of a group of Rotarians who were on a mission to help "Eradicate Polio by 2005" from the Earth. For a few days in mid-October, ninety-three Rotary volunteers traveled to Ghana, Africa and joined a door-to-door immunization effort targeting children five and under, we were put into teams that included a local Rotarian, Ghanaian volunteer and Rotaract students. These teams of several hundred trudged over open sewer canals running down residential streets, to safeguard a staggering 9,000 children from polio's devastation. Surprisingly, the children we treated were mostly eager to swallow the two little drops that would so casually remove them from harm's way. But, they especially liked to show off the spot of temporary dye on their thumbnail, which signaled their inoculation and attested their bravery—not to mention hailed their, usually first, experience with "Brunies" (whites). Sometimes a particularly curious child would sneak a touch of our hand to see if our 'white' would smudge. The children we encountered were playful, inquisitive and very grateful, which greatly added to our sense of service and fulfillment. Karolina and I are proud and privileged to have contributed a small part to making this major push toward the international goal of total polio eradication by 2005. We believe it is possible—we know it is imminent. And, God's grace will provide the hour for good intentions, a loving community spirit and the hard work of so many to prevail.

—Mark Perry
Club President
Visalia Breakfast Rotary Club
Visalia, California, USA

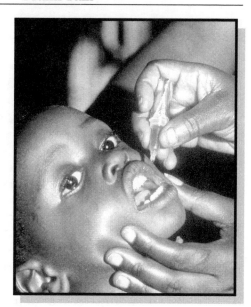

PolioPlus—"Rotary's Gift to the World"—has already immunized 2 billion children against polio, with the goal that the dreaded disease will be eradicated globally by 2005.

While PolioPlus is preventing new outbreaks of polio, Rotarians are also providing wheelchairs, job training, and restorative surgery to existing victims.

CHAPTER 6

What Difference Can One Person Make?

"**F**rank, you said something a while ago that triggered a thought in my mind. I don't want to be rude, but may I be honest with you?" asked Bob.

I wasn't sure what was coming, but I told him to go ahead.

"From what you've said, about owning a large company, to the cost of your prestigious club memberships and even from the quality of the clothes you're wearing, it's clear to me that you are not a man who lives on the poverty line. You talked about Rotary eliminating polio and traveling to help the needy in faraway countries. It is easy for rich people to do those things. I'm just one person, a middle-class, hardworking guy looking to get ahead, I *do* care about people less fortunate than me, but I can't see how one person can make a difference."

"Let me answer your question with a question: do you *want* to make a difference," I asked.

"Of course I do. I told you how I felt trapped between *wanting* to help and feeling *able* to help after seeing those people in the Philippines," he said. "But I don't see how one individual can do much at all. Look at the homeless people we see in our big cities. What can I do...give the guy enough money to buy a meal? What difference will that make? I can't educate him, I can't give him a job, and I can't treat him for alcoholism or mental illness. Neither can Sue, or Duncan. But that's where the problem lies. You see, we're not millionaire business people, we're not politicians, we're just ordinary people, and I don't see how a solitary ordinary person like me could solve anything."

"May I say something?" Duncan asked. "Bob, for much of my life, I felt the same way. I gave money to a few favorite charities. I participated in things at work, such as our annual fundraising campaign, but I never felt much of a connection between the checks I wrote and the needs my contributions addressed. I agree with you. I never thought one person could make a difference—until my retirement dinner."

"I didn't even *get* a retirement dinner," said Sue, with a rueful look.

"I must say, DuPro Chemical treats their retirees very well," Duncan continued. "But mine was different from others I've attended. Sure, there were a lot of jokes and a few touching reminiscences from people who'd worked with me during my 40 years there. Then the CEO spoke. He told how he had been asked to deliver the commencement address to the graduating class of some university the same afternoon, and then he had to think about what to say at my retirement dinner."

"What an interesting contrast, a commencement address and a retirement speech—on the same day," Sue observed.

"That was his opening comment, too," Duncan continued. "Then he said that his message was the same, only the audiences were different. He told the graduates to be all that they could be, to use their God-given talents not to conform to the crowd but to create something special—to leave the world a better place than they found it, starting that very day. Then he turned to me—I was right next to him at the head table—and talked to me as if we were the only two people in the room. He challenged me to do the same as those young kids that were just beginning their careers. He told me 'Not to rust out, but to wear out.'

"He told the story of a young man jogging down the beach early one morning and seeing an old fellow picking things up off the sand and throwing them out to sea. When he got closer, he saw that a storm tide had washed tens of thousands of starfish up on the beach overnight, and the receding tide was leaving them stranded. The old man was picking them up and casting them back into the water so the rising sun would not fry them. 'How can you expect to make any difference to so many thousands of starfish? The sun is already coming over the horizon,' the young man said. The old man said nothing, but hurried over to another beleaguered starfish stranded on the beach and hurled it out to sea. As he ran past the young jogger, he said, 'I made a difference to that one, didn't I?'

"Right there at the retirement dinner, I realized that I alone couldn't solve all the problems of the world. But I could make a difference to someone. That's when I also took my CEO's other piece of advice and decided not to sit in a rocking chair and 'rust out.' I volunteered at the hospital the very next day. Then about three months ago, I began reading books to the blind. I can't cure blindness, and I can't help the hundreds of thousands who already have it, but I know I'm making a difference to some people."

"That was compelling testimony," I said. "Now can you imagine being a member of a club that not only offered all the benefits we've discussed so far this afternoon, but where many of the members were as committed as you are to the ideal of service to humankind? Bob asked, 'Can one person make a difference?' Duncan says, 'Yes, you bet you can!' But what I'm stressing is, *imagine* how much of a difference we can make with a million Duncans. Duncan is the kind of person who will inspire members of many Rotary clubs to work in a similar fashion. A million people—and notice that I didn't pick the richest, most influential, most powerful person—I picked an ordinary man like Duncan. Imagine if we could harness his commitment to humanity and his passion for enthusiastic service—and multiply that one million times. *Then* could we make a difference?"

"There wouldn't be many starfish left on the beach," said Sue.

"*Exactly*," I agreed, with a smile. I had made my point! I had gotten my message across. "A wonderful Australian man named Clem Renouf—as humble a person as you could ever meet—loves to say, 'Rotary allows ordinary people to become extraordinary Rotarians.' Clem is known as the driving force that launched our PolioPlus campaign. One man had an idea. But good ideas die on the vine every day because there is nobody else around, or insufficient resources to nurture them. But Clem's good idea to immunize against polio all the children in one geographic region got picked up by another Rotarian, my fellow countryman, Dr. Carlos Canseco, who expanded the vision to eradicate the disease everywhere on earth. Because of their stature, one Rotarian had connections with a laboratory that donated vaccine, another had connections with international health agencies, yet another was so influential in Mexico that he was able to meet that country's president and sell him on the idea. Let's go back to Clem Renouf; *he* couldn't have persuaded the lab in Canada to donate the vaccine and would probably have never secured a private meeting with the president of Mexico, but his fellow Rotarians did. Do you see my point? First of all, many Rotarians are in positions of influence and can help make things happen—whether that Rotarian is the mayor of your town or an insider at the presidential palace. Second, taken individually, none of the people could have made a difference to the half-million children who died from polio each year. But when Clem in Australia and M.A.T Caparas in the Philippines and Carlos Canseco in Mexico and Herb Brown in the USA—and 1.2 million other Rotarians just like them—when *they* catch the vision and enthusiasm of that originator of the idea, watch out! Then you have an unstoppable force for good that can change the world.

"Rotarians accomplished a feat unmatched in human history. They have immunized two billion children so far. Several times they mobilized members, families, friends, coworkers to immunize 100 million children *in a single day* in places like India and Nigeria. We have totally eradicated polio from the Western Pacific, from most of Europe, from China, the entire Western Hemisphere, and Rotary's gift to the world is our pledge to have eradicated the scourge of polio from the face of the earth by 2005—our 100th anniversary. No individual, no government, not even the United Nations could accomplish such a miraculous achievement—but a group of motivated individuals united in Rotary's ideal of service will.

"One of the most amazing things about the success of Rotary is that it is achieved entirely by volunteers. It all starts because one Rotarian *wants* something to happen, not because some boss *tells* him or her to do it, or to fulfill a mission statement that's posted on a wall somewhere. Every successful project that Rotary has ever accomplished has begun at the grass roots level in the minds and hearts of individual Rotarians.

"One Rotarian back in 1912 was so disgusted with the rampant corruption and unethical business conduct that he wrote a Code of Business Ethics. Rotary adopted it, then promoted it to other business organizations, with the result that 145 national and international trade associations subsequently adopted similar ethical standards. Eighty years ago, one man, 'Daddy' Allen, was the visionary who started Rotary's work with crippled children. His idea soon spread to Rotary clubs around the world and ultimately was spun off to become what we today call the Easter Seals Society. Do you think Daddy Allen made a difference?"

"It's interesting that we should be talking about this," Sue interjected. "I was reading a book yesterday about the popularity of volunteerism in recent years, and the author quoted Margaret Mead, the anthropologist. Her quote so touched me that I copied it into my daily planner. She said, 'Never doubt that a group of committed, dedicated individuals can change the world. Indeed, that is the only thing that ever has.' I felt those words were a personal challenge to me, in a way affirming my decision to volunteer at my church preschool."

"That's wonderful," I agreed. "Now imagine how good you'll feel when in addition to helping *those* kids, you can have a nice meal with your new Rotary friends and help millions of kids, kids every bit as precious to their parents as the ones in your church school. We have projects in India to dig wells so they can have safe drinking water, immunization programs in Africa, literacy projects in Asia, avoidable blindness schemes in Latin America, tutoring groups in America's inner cities."

"But are individual Rotarians involved with those projects, or is it like some religious organizations where they're constantly badgering you for money?" asked Bob.

"Actually, Rotary has no requirement that members support its programs," I explained. "The headquarters publicizes the different service opportunities, but it is entirely up to individual Rotarians as to whether, and how much, they want to give. But while you won't have to give, I'm sure you'll soon *want* to participate. Rotarians can now go to countries that are holding national immunization days and can participate in the operation. Rotarians in New Jersey have built orphanages in Romania; California Rotarians who are plastic and orthopedic surgeons now make frequent trips to developing countries to perform restorative surgery on crippled children. French dentists take their talents to Vietnam, British members have helped establish fish farms in Bangladesh, Swedish Rotarian surgeons have numerous projects in Africa, Japanese Rotarians have year-round service projects in Nepal—and every one of these missions was an idea first germinated by a solitary Rotarian, but brought to fruition by . . . Sue, what were those words by Margaret Mead?"

"A group of committed, dedicated individuals... that can change the world."

"That's it! That defines Rotarians. You see, joining a Rotary club is a bit like going to a restaurant. Some people order the chef's choice, others order just the soup and the salad, others order something from each menu category."

"And some of us start with dessert!" said Sue, patting her stomach.

"Precisely. And so it is with Rotary. Some nibble a little, others dive in and try everything on the menu. I know one Rotarian who initiated a local summer school program for handicapped children, started his club bulletin and wrote it every week, launched a project that airlifted relief supplies to victims of natural disasters, and started a computer training program with 25 computers that equipped orphans in Eastern Europe with job skills. But he was no better a member than the person he sat next to at Rotary each week who was not as 'hungry' for service, because that member helped the club in other ways."

"But Frank, that first guy sounded like he made Rotary his full-time job. I don't think I could ever give that much time to Rotary, or any organization," objected Bob.

"Well let me tell you about one of his goodwill adventures," I continued. "During a lull in the Lebanese civil war, David motivated his club to collect thousands of toys to give to children in Beirut who had been orphaned by 17 years of war. Through another connection, an airline donated the cargo space—which itself was an $18,000 gift. But when he arrived at Beirut Airport, he found it under the control of a rebel militia, and they demanded a $5,000 cash bribe before he could get through customs with the toys."

"That's awful!" said Sue. "Imagine going through all that work only to have it ruined. Did he pay them the money?"

"No. He had contacted the Beirut Rotary Club in advance, and they had a Rotarian at the airport waiting for him. When David told him what was happening, the man spoke in Arabic to the militia, asking them to hold the shipment safely until the next day, inferring that he would return with the money. But the next morning, the Lebanese Rotarian drove David across town to meet a fellow club member, who was country representative for UNICEF. He quickly did some creative paperwork and reconsigned the shipment to the UN—making it diplomatic cargo, *untouchable by anybody*! He even sent two UN trucks out to the airport, and within hours, they were distributing the toys to orphaned children all over Beirut. You see, David alone could never have made that project a success. But when you added the enthusiasm of his fellow club members, the contacts one of them had with the airline, the prestige of Rotary's name, the international network that enabled him to have a fellow Rotarian waiting for him at the airport, and then *that* member's local network of connections to call on in a crisis—*then* you have proof that, through Rotary, one person can make a difference.

"So you can be the generator of ideas or you can be the worker bee that says, 'I'll give you a hand here' or 'I'll help in such-and-such a way there.'"

"And you don't think that I'm too old to get started," asked Duncan.

Before I could answer, Bob, uncharacteristically, jumped into the conversation. "You're not too old for the blind people you read books to.

You're not too old to make a difference when you volunteer at the hospital, are you?"

Duncan pursed his lips and nodded thoughtfully. I wanted to jump in and tell Duncan about one of my personal passions that the Rotary Foundation has been emphasizing lately: the cause of avoidable blindness. I wanted to tell him about seeing an old man in India being led around by his grandson because he was blind. The little boy brought him into a Rotary eye camp where for less than $100 we perform cataract surgery that restores the sight of three people. But I decided to take a more philosophical approach.

"What will your tombstone read?" I asked.

"Oh, Frank! Now there's a morbid thought," Sue complained. "How on earth did we get onto the subject of tombstones?"

"Since you're the one objecting, let me direct the question to you then," I said, looking directly into her eyes. "Do we all agree that one day, we all will die?" They nodded cautiously, as if I was about to trap them. But I really wasn't.

"When that time comes, no matter when it happens, no matter your age, your religion, bank balance or social standing, your graves will probably be marked with a tombstone. For a hundred or maybe two hundred or more years to come, the only thing that passers-by will associate with the time you spent on this earth will be what's on your tombstone. Engraved into the marble will be your name, the date you were born, a dash, and the date you died. I submit to you the most important part of that tombstone is the dash, what you did between the day you were born and the day you died.

"So Duncan, Sue, Bob—it's never too late to start working on your dash. You asked whether one *ordinary* person can make a difference, implying that only the rich or famous could do so. Let me ask you something: can you name the five wealthiest people in the world? Can you name the quarterbacks of the last five winning Superbowl teams? How about naming the last five winners of the Miss Universe contest? Or the "Best Actor" winners of the last five Academy Awards?" I waited for almost four minutes, and even when they consulted among themselves, my three friends could not answer a single one of my questions.

"Those people were the best in their fields, and yet, once the applause has died down, their accolades are forgotten and their awards tarnish and fade into oblivion. Now let me give you another test. List a few teachers who helped your journey through school. Name five friends who have helped you during difficult times. Name five people who have taught you something worthwhile in life. Name five more who have made you feel special." For more than 20 minutes, first Sue, then Duncan, and finally Bob talked about people from each of those categories.

"You see," I said, when they had finished. "The people who made a difference in *your* lives were not the rich ones, not the famous names, nor people who received prestigious awards. They were real people who took the time to pass on their love and compassion and friendship. And all these years later, those simple acts of kindness made such a difference that you can still remember their names and faces.

"Now *you* can pass on what they gave to you. You can make a difference to people who will lengthen the dash on your tombstone—and you can have fun doing so. And I know the organization that can help you get started."

I was fortunate enough to be chosen a GSE Team Leader to Jordan in 1997. While there one of the Rotary Clubs challenged us to do a Matching Grant with "The Home of Hope" in Zarqa, Jordan. The challenge was accepted. Following the completion of raising the money, doing the paperwork, ordering the equipment, the decision was made to go back to Jordan and be there for the delivery of the equipment in 1998. However things never quite happen the way we anticipate, so I was able to arrange for the delivery of a few things by UPS. Upon my arrival in Amman, and after a few days of jet lag rest, the Amman Jerish Rotary Club President personally drove me over to the home, where several other members and some of the members of the board of the Home plus some parents of the children met us. Following a brief tour, singing by the children and a few speeches, we were ready to have tea and sweets. It all came together when a mother of one of the children came up to me and said "Thank You for what you have done!" with tears in her eyes. All I did was tell their story to other Rotary Clubs and other groups. To think the little that I did made such a difference for these children in Jordan! What a heartwarming experience. I thank Rotary for the wonderful opportunity to make a difference.

—Marlene "Moe" Otte
Past District Governor
Sauk Centre Rotary Club, MN. USA

CHAPTER 7

Now What?

"I 'm really moved by what you've told us today, Frank," said Sue. "It makes sense to me. I think Rotary's networking opportunities could help me grow my business, and if you represent the new generation of Rotarians, I certainly would like to include them among my friends. How do you get in to a Rotary club? Are there secret rituals or anything?"

"Sue . . . we're not a college fraternity with hazing ceremonies and secret handshakes, and we don't sacrifice live animals when we induct new members," I laughed. "Do you have a business card? In fact, why don't we all exchange business cards?" For a few minutes confusion reigned while people searched for their cards and then passed them back and forth, finally accomplishing the task of each having the other three people's cards.

I remembered something a sales trainer had told my own sales staff a few years ago when he conducted a seminar for us in Mexico. "The reason most salespeople fail is because they never ask for the order," he had said. I asked him to explain what he meant and he elaborated: "Time and again, salespeople do a good job of greeting the customer and building rapport, a great job of explaining the product features, but then fail to close the sale." I realized that many of us make the same mistake in Rotary. We tell prospective members *who* we are and *what* we do, but then we don't close the loop by inviting them to join. "Why is that?" I have often wondered. The fear of rejection in case the person says "No," perhaps? Embarrassment at moving from the conversation mode to the more confrontational selling mode? Or is it just because as leaders in our organizations we tend to feel in control of things, and when we ask an open question such as "Will you join my Rotary club?" we are no longer certain of the answer? It is probably a combination of all three reasons. Regardless, I thought, I've made that mistake before; I am not going to make it again.

"In the past three hours, I feel as if I've come to know the three of you quite well," I began. "It seemed as if we were from four different worlds when we first met, but as time passed, we've found so many qualities and values in one person that were shared by the others. I think you would be wonderful Rotarians, and I also believe Rotary would be good for you, on both a personal and professional level. Duncan, would you be interested in joining Rotary?"

"You know, Frank, I believe I would," he said. "I wish I had joined it years ago when I was first invited. But I'm not going to make excuses this time. The truth is, I don't have a lot of close friends, and I see Rotary as a source of good fellowship for me. It sounds like it will be a wonderful resource for me when I travel, and maybe I can help out with local community service projects since my time is now my own. In fact, maybe I could recruit some of the Rotarians to come read to the blind folks at the nursing home."

"Sue? If a Rotary club in your area has an opening for somebody in your type of business, would you consider joining?"

"What day would they meet?" she asked. "Because I really don't want to give up my Monday golf outings, and the church preschool needs me on Thursday mornings."

"That shouldn't be an issue," I assured her. "Do you live in a rural village or a big city?"

"Neither," she replied. "I live in Medfield, which is a town of 18,000. It's a suburb of a much larger city."

"I'm sure there is a Rotary club in Medfield, but if they meet at noon on Mondays, there's bound to be another club nearby that meets at a different time. I know that in my district I can visit a Rotary club that meets on any weekday, morning, noon, or evening—and all of them are within a half-hour of my home or office. Rotary changed its membership rules a few years ago and you no longer have to join the club in the town in which you live or work. Do you have access to the Internet?"

"Yes," she said.

"If you go to the Rotary Website, www.rotary.org, and click on the button that says 'Administrative

Services.' When that page appears, you click on 'Where Clubs Meet,' then type in your city. It will display the day, time, and location of your town's Rotary club meetings. If you then click on the four-digit district number it will display the meeting details of every club in the area, along with a contact telephone number for each club.

"If you do not have Web access, you can call Rotary headquarters in Evanston, Illinois, at 847.866.3000, or check with your local library or city hall. They usually know when and where each Rotary club meets. So do the important hotels in any town.

"Bob, my last victim...I mean, candidate! I can tell from your voice tone and your body language that you are a very process-oriented guy who thinks things through carefully before coming to a decision. But I also feel that I have seen in you an emotional side that cares deeply about injustice, poverty, and the suffering of humankind. Would you consider joining Rotary?"

Bob sighed and looked out of the window, avoiding eye contact as he considered his answer. "I believe it would help me develop career skills," he began. "That would be a good thing. You were also very perceptive about almost all of my friends being people I work with at eData, and I can see how Rotary would give me the opportunity to expand my circle of friends and business contacts in the outside world. But I see value in another area, too. After what Duncan shared with us, I realize that I need to change my priorities. There has to be more to life than work, sleep, work, sleep, work, buy new toys, work, and sleep. I don't really feel part of our community, and I think Rotary would change that. I like the idea of getting my hands dirty with volunteer work, and if Sarah and I could volunteer on some project together, I think she'd really like that. We'd be helping others *and* spending quality time together. If there were times when my workload prevented me from participating directly, we could support others who were doing Rotary' work, I guess. Still, I am concerned about the people in the club—what if the club in *my* town has a bunch of morons instead of a bunch of live wires in it? And what if they are totally inflexible and jump all over me if I miss a couple of meetings?"

"If you could be satisfied with the answers to those two questions, would you join?" I asked.

"Yes, Frank, I believe I would," he replied.

"Then here's what I suggest you do. First, talk with your boss or even your boss's boss. Tell him or her that you are considering joining Rotary, the world's largest network of business leaders dedicated to serving their communities. Say how we met and how you've realized that Rotary membership would enhance your leadership skills and networking abilities for potential clients and future employees. And as eData's representative in Rotary, it will express the company's image of being civic minded—a good corporate citizen. Ask them if they would support your membership, either by paying your dues or by allowing you to attend the meetings a little beyond your normal lunch hour."

"Or both!" he added, with a broad smile.

"Or both!" I agreed. "If your boss gives it his or her blessing, you've just eliminated that concern about attending a meeting in the middle of the day, haven't you?" He nodded.

"If your boss is short sighted and doesn't encourage you that way, you probably should pick a Rotary club that meets for breakfast or dinner. Follow the same procedure I just outlined for Sue: www.rotary.org, Administrative Services, Where Clubs Meet. Enter your town, and then click on the district number for nearby clubs. I suggest that you go visit several clubs in your area. You can either call the club secretary or president first, or simply drop in on the club at its regular meeting time. Ask the president or secretary if they have an opening for someone in your field, tell them you sometimes have crises that could prevent you from maintaining perfect attendance and ask if that would be a problem for them. Ask about their active club projects, about how they could use you—and Sarah. Compare the camaraderie and fellowship of the clubs you visit and then pick the one you've enjoyed the most. Every Rotary club is autonomous, and I have long said that Rotary clubs are like people: some are more fun than others, some are energetic, others are slower moving, some are enthusiastic, some are less so. So out of 30,000 clubs if you find one that seems to be just plodding along waiting for someone like you to give it new life, you've got two choices: either go to the next club, or join the first club where you might be the spark that ignites them into new, vibrant action. That might be the one that changes your life, and gives you the opportunity to change the lives of countless others."

"Ladies and gentlemen, in approximately two minutes we will be arriving at Central Station. This will be the final stop for this train. Please check around you and in the overhead rack for all personal belongings, and remain seated until the train has come to a complete stop. Thank you for riding with us today."

"What perfect timing," said Duncan, after the announcement had ended.

"It sure is—and right on time, too," I affirmed. "Bob, did I answer all your questions?

"You did. And I will follow up on your suggestion," he promised.

The train stopped and we stepped onto the platform. "Each Rotary International president chooses a theme for his year," I said. "My theme is, *Create Awareness and Take Action.* I'm so glad we've had this opportunity to get to know one another these last few hours. It seems a long time ago that you were all throwing those nasty inaccurate stereotypes about Rotary at me. So I hope I've been able to *Create Awareness* of what Rotary *really* is. But now it's up to each of you to *Take Action.* If you truly want to start working on what that dash on your tombstone will represent, you'll take action to join Rotary as soon as you get home."

"This *is* my home town," said Duncan. "I'm going to take action today."

"I'm so glad to have met you all," said Bob, extending his hand to each of us. "It's been an inspiring journey for me."

"Me too," said Sue, giving each of us a farewell hug. "But what excites me most is the feeling that the best part of the journey is yet to come."

Rotary offers a code of ethics, though it is not a denomination. Rotary is a benevolent fellowship, but it is not a fraternity. Rotary can be a way of life, but it is not a religion. Rotary improves the quality of living in many homes, but it is not just another hometown club. Rotary encourages members to do vocational upgrades, but it is not an employment agency. Rotary offers the opportunity to better understand other businesses, but it is not just a networking organization. Rotary offers a platform to share ideas and better forms of business while eating, but it is not just a luncheon club. Rotary is a humanitarian time saver, not an organization that consumes valuable time. Rotary is an opportunity to share, not a restricted group.

—Robert Lee Ellis
Past District Governor
Bellaire/SW Houston Rotary Club
Houston, Texas, USA

There are no such things as strangers in Rotary—only friends we have yet to meet. At International Assemblies and Conventions, Rotarians and their families from 199 countries meet and enjoy the fellowship.

These children are enjoying the results of a Rotary project that dug deep wells and installed pumps—thus providing safe, clean drinking water for the first time in the village's history.

Why People Like You Joined Rotary

During my year as president of Rotary International, I realized the Internet could become a valuable communication tool for Rotary. We are a global organization composed of 1.2 million Rotarians in 30,000 clubs throughout 199 countries and geographic regions. The sun literally never sets on the world of Rotary for there is a club meeting taking place, somewhere on earth, every minute of every day.

I know why *I* joined Rotary, but why did the other people join? I decided to ask them. In just a couple of weeks after I invited Rotarians to submit their reasons for joining our organization to the www.frankdevlyn.org Website, over 1,000 members had sent in their reasons. The following is a sample of those submissions. To read the entire list of unedited testimonials from Rotarians around the world, go to:

www.frankdevlyn.org
or
www.rotary.org.

* * * * *

In a world filled with hatred, Rotary has a message of love; in a world filled with only promises, Rotary gives service—service without any selfish motive. In a diverse and disintegrating world, Rotary highlights the sense of unity; among the multitude of takers, Rotary teaches us to give, for there is always joy in giving. Joining Rotary can really make one's life meaningful. Some of the most satisfying experiences in the world may not be expressed in words; they can only be felt by a true human heart.

Eno Chodup Panlook, Rotarian,
Rotary Club of Kalimpong, W. B., India

Email: panlook@dte.vsnl.net.in

* * * * *

Why join Rotary? We all know that Philippines is one of the countries that has the highest level of poverty. During my early years as a youth I had always felt bad for the less fortunate. I had always dreamed of putting a shelter for some of these, especially children that have no home. I thought that some day I could be able to try to solve some of these problems, but as I got older I felt that this dream may not become a reality. So when I was invited to Rotary and saw some of the Rotary projects, I believed that in some way this could help me take action in my concern for our less fortunate brothers. I joined Rotary in February 1995 and went on to serve my club as Community Service director, president elect, and in 1999, and president. In line with the question "Why join Rotary?" when I recruit new members I always tell the new members that the first priority is to serve our less fortunate brothers and sisters. Fellowship and business will follow.

IPP Sunil Sitlani, Past Club President,
Rotary Club of Pasay West, Pasay City, Philippines

Email: promovis@pworld.net.ph

* * * * *

I feel that this is the best organization on the globe which serves the community in almost every field of life, be it literacy, health, social problems of a community—and now with the Rapid Disaster Relief committee, to meet the challenges of natural calamities. It also gives the best opportunity to develop friendship in your city, country and internationally, developing organizational, oration and leadership skills.

**Dr. J. N. Gurtu, Club President,
Rotary Club of Calcutta Victoria, Calcutta-Bengal-India**

Email: gurtu@doctor.com

* * * * *

My wife and I were driving home from a Rotary function one evening. Just quietly talking as a husband and wife often do, when she made an observation that I really hadn't made about myself yet. She said that my heart has led me to Rotary. That I had found that thing in life I had been missing. I had the need to feel that my actions were accomplishing something and doing some good in this world.

I spent a lot of time being frustrated before joining the Rockland Rotary club. I had been a member of other civic groups that spent so much time bickering among the members that progress was kept to a slow standstill. In Rotary I found a large group of people that would put their energy and willpower towards a common goal and made great things happen. Every fundraiser and project we undertake in Rotary has a benefit to somebody. And that somebody may be in a war torn country overseas or a family in need the next street over.

**Leni S. Gronros, Club President,
Rotary Club of Rockland, Rockland, Maine USA**

Email: leni@midcoast.com

* * * * *

Rotary is an opportunity for me to serve my community within an established international organization. Fellowship with professionals from various walks of life, from my own country or expatriate residents is a major plus.

**Joe F. Boulos, Past Club President,
Beirut-Cosmopolitan Rotary Club, Beirut, Lebanon**

Email: rightangle@inco.com.lb

* * * * *

I am a Rotarian because the values of Rotary are my values. Attendance at Rotary meetings and participation in Rotary projects remind me to be the type of person I want to be—involved in improving my community, promoting high ethical standards in my profession, and helping to improve living standards in disadvantaged regions of the world.

**David C. Williams, Past District Governor,
Rotary Club of Wilmington, CA USA**

Email: uspswilm1@juno.com

* * * * *

Gracias a Rotary, mis esfuerzos por hacer de este mundo un mundo mejor, se están multiplicando. Ya no me siento sólo. Me siento acompañado, entendido, apoyado y cómodo de haber decidido este estilo de vida como testimonio hacia mí y los demás. Por eso invito a tódos quienes participan de Rotary, hacer conciencia y tomar acción por obtener un mundo mejor. Que Dios los bendiga a tódos.

**Fernando Aguirre Palacios, Rotarian,
Rotary Club of Guayaquil, Ecuador**

Email: faguirre@ec.telconet.net

* * * * *

I joined Rotary because someone I respected asked me and because I wanted to get to know more people in a community that was new to me. Very often a club has members who are state and local government officials, doctors, educators, building contractors, bankers, and lawyers. It can be personally very advantageous for a businessperson to get to know these people. I believe that the reasons for joining Rotary are very different from the reasons why people stay in Rotary.

**Timothy P. Morsani, Rotarian,
Rotary Club of Carson City, Nevada, USA**

Email: Lmorsani@aol.com

* * * * *

Rotary membership has broadened my life personally, socially, professionally, vocationally, and educationally. Personally, 1 have met hundreds of people, many of whom 1 now call my friends. Socially, Rotary has given me access to a wide range of social experiences with a sense of belonging to a special group of people who contribute to others both locally and internationally. Professionally, Rotary has allowed me to grow in my professional skills while sharing my expertise with others. Vocationally Rotary has connected me to a wide range of vocations broadening my understanding of business and community. Educationally, 1 have been exposed to professional development on a weekly basis through contact with fellow Rotarians, guest speakers, specific projects and community involvement. 1 am proud to be a Rotarian. 1 will be forever grateful to my proposer, and 1 look forward to the future as a Rotarian.

**Ros Bradbury, Rotarian,
Rotary Club of Bendigo, Victoria, Australia**

Email: Ros_Bradbury@aep.salvationarmy.org

* * * * *

I read an article from the *Wall Street Journal* several years ago which pointed out that corporations spend thousands of dollars a year training their executives. The article suggested that corporations should consider organizations like Rotary where, at less of an expense, their future leaders could gain people skills, management skills, networking skills, and at the same time serve humanity. I know I have experienced considerable personal growth thanks to Rotary. I encourage my top managers not just to join Rotary, but also to become Rotarians.

John William Nugent, Rotarian,
Rotary Club of Westchester, CA.USA

Email: jnnugent@hotmail.com

* * * * *

Membership in Rotary will enable you to share the wealth of the first-world country with the less fortunate countries in a direct and controllable manner. Rotary is founded on private enterprise and initiative and must be the largest organisation that can achieve this through private enterprise.

James Kenneth Emery, Club President, Rotary Club
of Glenelg, Adelaide, South Australia, Australia

Email: heatherjim@adelaide.on.net

* * * * *

As a woman traveling out of town for business (public relations and marketing), Rotary meetings are a true blessing for stress-free fellowship and a true insight into the community.

Cassandra Consorto Schultz, Rotarian,
Paoli, Malvern, Berwyn Rotary Club, Pennsylvania, USA

Email: consortocass@aol.com

* * * * *

I joined Rotary quite a few years ago, but that didn't make me a Rotarian. Only when I held in my arms a poor child waiting to have his cleft lip operated on by the Medical Professionals of Rotaplast, an organization supported by Rotary Clubs and private donations and when, just a couple of hours later, I brought the same child to the recovery room, and I witnessed the instant miracle that changed the disfiguring frown of this little, trembling piece of humanity into a radiant smile, then I BECAME A ROTARIAN. We must tell our prospective members that Rotary is so far more than a place to enjoy fellowship. It is an opportunity, for which we all should be grateful, to change lives, and in doing so, to change our own.

Renato Piombi, Rotarian,
Belmont Rotary Club, Belmont, CA USA

Email: rpiombi@pacbell.net

* * * * *

I have been a member of a Rotary club for over twenty years, in two countries, even though I am only just 50. Rotary is not an old man's club. Rotary has given me balance in my life in allowing me to help others in a productive way. I've made many dear friends, and many business contacts with whom I can deal with trust, because as Rotarians they are bound by a code of behaviour. I have nominated friends, business colleagues, and clients, for Rotary membership. They have all found the same things as me. When I moved to Singapore from Australia one of the first things I did was to join a local Rotary club. I felt incomplete without it.

Keith William Callinan, Past Club President,
Rotary Club of Singapore, Singapore.

Email: callinan@singnet.com.sg

* * * * *

I joined Rotary for no particular reason other than I was invited, and was curious as to what took place. However, after a few months in a friendly atmosphere, I began to understand what Rotary was all about, and concluded that I should have joined much sooner than I did. Getting involved in projects was something that I was skeptical of; however, when I saw what the project was and the end results, i.e. help in the local and worldwide community, I could not wait to get involved, and after completion, I look around for the next idea. Rotary to me is working in tandem with other Rotarians, the community, and sometimes other organizations. Satisfaction is the key and one wears a certain pride after helping someone else. Rotary to me is not just serving in a charitable way, but also includes vocational services, and of course the weekly luncheon, which in our club is also a fun time. To sum it all up, Rotary to me is service, fun and camaraderie, whether at the local club, district or international level.

Robert Maxwell, Rotarian,
Rotary Club of Etobicoke, Toronto, Ontario, Canada

Email: bmaxwell@pkdouglass.com

*   *   *   *   *

I joined for all the wrong reasons 12 years ago—to network with other businesses—but stayed for all the right reasons. I receive more from this organization than I could ever hope to return— the fellowship and pride are enormously rewarding. Giving back to Rotary has become very important to me—within my local club and nationally, and I work faithfully to attain that goal.

Jacquelyn Kahn, Past Club President,
Lewiston/Auburn Rotary Club, Lewiston, Maine USA

Email: jkahn829@aol.com

*   *   *   *   *

My husband, Mike, joined Rotary because a good friend suggested it would increase our social and business contacts in the area, enable us to contribute something to the community in a more effective way, and enjoy the many activities of the club. While the above was all true, one of the main effects was that setting aside one night a week from a busy work and family life gave him an interest outside of work. He began a pattern of setting time aside for activities that added variety to both our lives. We have made lifelong friends through Rotary, as well as seeing many projects on which we spent time coming to fulfillment. It is amazing what a small group of people, working together, can achieve while at the same time, enjoying themselves. I would recommend Rotary to all workaholics; Mike's meeting night became his "cone of escape" from work. He died quite unexpectedly some 15 years after joining Sutherland Club near Sydney, and with the support I received from the club, plus the pattern of many years going to Rotary "things", when a local club asked me to join I was pleased to continue my association and the lifestyle of Rotary.

Elaine Lytle, Past Club President,
Como Jannali Rotary Club, Sydney, NSW, Australia

Email: spinco@tig.com.au

* * * * *

A big reason for joining Rotary is my children. I want them to have an understanding of selflessness and to learn about the spirit of service. I want them to see that we have a good life in this part of the world and that we have lots, and therefore have lots to give.

Gina Brosseau, Rotarian,
Rotary Club of Red Deer East, Red Deer, Alberta, Canada

Email: gina @business-dynamics.ca

* * * * *

The reasons to join Rotary are contained in four words . . . Friendship: It is worldwide and immediate no matter which country one is visiting. Service: It is the pleasure one gets from helping others in your community without thought of remuneration. International: Rotary is truly an International Organisation with clubs in 199 countries. Peace: Through The Rotary Foundation programs are available for each and every person to make a real impact in the world as we all strive for a better more peaceful one.

**Robert S. Scott, Past Director of
Rotary International, Cobourg Rotary Club,
Cobourg Ontario Canada**

Email: bobscott@eagle.ca

*   *   *   *   *

Rotary provides the opportunity to make a difference. We are able to help people both internationally and locally. Rotary is a well-respected organization with an established track record of doing great things for many people. Rotary also provides an oasis from the busy week, a place where I can enjoy the company of other Rotarians and guests, share a meal, fellowship, a laugh and learn a thing or two. Rotary also provides a worldwide bond to other Rotarians. Whether I go 20 miles or 2000 I know I can find a Rotary club and feel welcome. I can tell from talking to the seasoned members that Rotary has been a very special organization to them.

**Paul K. Page, Rotarian,
Hornell Rotary Club, Hornell, NY, USA**

Email: pkpage@infoblvd.net

*   *   *   *   *

Rotary has enriched my life and the lives of my whole family. My circle of friends has expanded through Rotary membership, both in the local community and internationally. What a joy it is to open my e-mail every day and find friendly messages from Holland, Honduras, India, Mexico, and Ghana. I experience satisfaction in using my professional skills on behalf of Rotary, primarily in the area of training. I am fulfilling my desire to "give back" for all of the blessings life has given me. I am so fortunate to have time, health, and resources to devote to Rotary service.

**Carolyn A. Schuetz, Past District Governor,
Hayward South Rotary Club, Hayward, California, USA**

Email: CSandLB@cs.com

* * * * *

Rotary is perhaps the only non-political, non-religious world organisation that does not discriminate between sex and personal standing of an individual. This organisation has earned unparalleled credibility in the eyes of governments and the general public.

Additionally, Rotary offers an unique opportunity of personality growth, since each dedicated member can easily get involved in working at the club level soon after joining as a new Rotarian. Such involvement offers growth of leadership quality, public speaking, and tolerance for each other; all this, while one continues to spend one's time, energy, and resources towards helping weaker sections of society for a better world.

**Vishnu Dhandhania, Club President,
Calcutta Metropolitan Rotary Club, Calcutta, WB, India**

Email: bally@vsnl.com

* * * * *

Before my good friend shared Rotary with me in 1979, my world was incomplete. I never understood the true meaning of service to mankind and fellowship with others.

Since then, I have had the opportunity of attending several Rotary assemblies and conferences, and meeting with interesting and delightful people from varied ethnic and social backgrounds. I have had the privilege of serving the disabled, senior citizens, the youth and the poor, giving my life a new meaning.

Today, I am much happier. I have maintained 100% attendance for 22 years and have had the honour of serving in various capacities including club president, assistant governor and now district governor nominee.

My Rotary experience has given me great satisfaction. I love Rotary and am proud to be a Rotarian. You will too.

Keith I. Daley, District Governor Nominee,
Rotary Club of Kingston, Kingston, Jamaica

Email: vmps@wtjam.net

* * * * *

Rotary connects me with a bigger world beyond my day-to-day activities. Through its motto "Service Above Self," Rotary allows me to meet and work with business people of like mind to help improve the plight of others in my community, my country, and the world. Through friendship and purpose, it connects me to something greater than what I am personally. Everyone wins.

David Glass, Rotarian,
Rotary Club of Kitchener, Kitchener, Ontario, Canada

Email: david@corepathsystems.com

* * * * *

Being a member of Rotary over the last four years has added new dimensions in my life. The values for which Rotary stands—Service Above Self—gives me greater ability to be Christ's hands and feet (on earth) than I could be by myself. As a member of Rotary, I am provided the opportunity to join an international membership whose purpose is to improve world peace and understanding. In my local club, the community projects *do* make a difference. A deep sense of pride grows each day. I am grateful to be a Rotarian.

Karen Tweed, Club President,
Bolivar Rotary Club, Bolivar, MO, USA

Email: ktweed@microcore.net

* * * * *

I initially joined Rotary for networking purposes. I soon realized the real meaning of Rotary. I've always tried to achieve a balance in giving to the community at home and internationally. Rotary does that. We have projects locally and join funds through the matching grants for international projects. The friends I have made in the past six years are friends for life. As one of five females in a group of 40 men I am treated with respect and we have a great time at our lunches. If I'm not feeling too cheery I know when I go to a Rotary lunch I get an incredible lift from the other members. I now do business with most of the members, but that is from developing the trusting relationships over time. If you are a female looking at Rotary, don't hesitate. Join today and don't just be a member, be a Rotarian.

Teresa Marshall, Rotarian,
North Delta Rotary Club, Delta, BC, Canada

Email: tmarshal@axionet.com

* * * * *

When I initially joined Rotary I developed public-speaking skills that I did not have the chance to achieve in my workplace. Since then my self-confidence has increased so much that I feel a debt to Rotary, to work harder for Rotary.

Over the past nearly 20 years I've experienced Rotary internationally and in every avenue of service, and the things I've learnt from this could not have been duplicated in any other forum.

I enjoy the fellowship of Rotary and the immense rewards one has after completing a successful project.

Kenneth Kay, Past Club President,
Randburg Rotary Club, Johannesburg, GP, South Africa

Email: kenneth.kay@mweb.co.za

* * * * *

Sin pasar de largo: Considero que una de las preocupaciones principales en mi vida y la de muchos ha sido el no pasar por ésta vida sin dejar algo positivo a las generaciones futuras, sin dejar huella con alguna aportación a nuestros hijos y su generación contribuyendo a mejorar nuestro mundo, ayudando a acortar la brecha entre el hambre y la bonanza, entre riqueza y pobreza (también de espíritu). Una manera de hacerlo es a través de Rotary, que tiene muy bien definidas las áreas de apoyo a los más necesitados, a través de sus avenidas de servicio, además de fomentar grandes amistades entre sus miembros y buenas relaciones entre los países.

Manuel Cantú, Rotarian,
Club Rotario Chihuahua amigo, Chihuahua, Mexico

Email: manuel.cantu@mx.marposs.com

* * * * *

I don't think there is anything in my life, besides my family, that has given me as many warm, good feelings as Rotary. The fellowship and the giving ethic of fellow Rotarians is without equal. When I see a stranger wearing a Rotary pin, it brings an instant smile to my face. There is a certain pride among Rotarians. It's in knowing that the four avenues of service that we follow are the basis of our motto "Service Above Self." We are all better by subscribing to, and believing in it.

John C. Brooks, District Governor, Rotary Club of Grosse Pointe, Grosse Pointe, Michigan, USA

Email: dgov2000@att.net

* * * * *

Through Rotary I bring hope, making a difference for men, women, and children, giving them an opportunity for a better life. Children have books in the school library to read. Underprivileged families are given food, clothing and shelter. Precious drops of polio vaccine are placed in the mouth of a child. Hopeless dreams turn into brighter realities; along the way I develop lifelong friendships with Rotarians. Rotary is Service, Fellowship, People, Family. This is why I am a Rotarian.

Carol A. Wylie, Past District Governor, Dominguez/Carson Rotary Club, Carson, CA U.S.A.

Email: cwylie@roycorp.com

* * * * *

Rotary provides an ideal forum for meeting interesting and talented people from all walks of life with whom one can work for a better tomorrow.

Yousuf Shahid, Rotarian, Rotary Club of Karachi Cosmopolitan, Karachi, Pakistan

Email: yousufshahid@hotmail.com

* * * * *

When interviewing prospective members I ask, "Have you had leadership experience?" Regardless of the answer the response is the same. In Rotary we learn to lead. If we arrive with leadership skills there are immediate opportunities to apply our leadership. If we feel the need for instruction we learn from doing. This atmosphere of service never ends. We grow and share our development with others to achieve levels of service that no individual can reach alone.

Ernest T. Bullock, Rotarian,
Penfield Rotary Club, Penfield, NY, USA

Email: ernest@rochester.rr.com

* * * * *

WHY I AM A ROTARIAN? What attracted me first was the strong fellowship at my Rotary club. I was astounded at the warm friendly welcome I received. Attending Rotary for Thursday lunch came as a welcome break during the busy week; I felt fresher and sharper for the break. Like everyone else in a new growing business, work is busy, intense, and consumes almost every waking moment. As the months went by I came to appreciate the company of my peers. The opportunity to mix and socialise in a relaxed environment has become a cornerstone to my Rotary experience. I get a strong sense of pride being part of a group that does so much for the community. When I see news items featuring Rotary at work I feel that in some small way, I am helping make the world a better place.

David Bennett, Rotarian,
Belmont Rotary Club, Western Australia

Email: daveb@space.net.au

* * * * *

Businesswomen have a lot to give to Rotary International. We raise families, organize households, act as everyone's social director and, therefore, bring commitment and organization to the Rotary clubs we join. What's in it for us? We find our "family" now including others throughout the world. Talk about your extended family! I now have friends in Mexico, Brazil, England, and Thailand, and I have only met these people in the last five years.

**Bernadette Julich, Past Club President,
Sunrise Rotary Club, Glenwood Springs, Colorado, USA**

Email: julich@coloradomtn.edu

* * * * *

I strive to make the world a better place. Trying to achieve this as a single individual is a rather terrifying and daunting experience. Being part of a large organisation like Rotary means that each member, worldwide, strives to make the world a better place. There IS strength in numbers. We *do* make a difference. Joining Rotary was the best thing I have done with my life.

**Nina Venjakob, Rotarian, Parktown Excalibur
Rotary Club, Johannesburg, South Africa**

Email: nina@global.co.za

* * * * *

Joining Rotary leads to lifelong friendships, improved organizational skills, a new sense of personal purpose, and a vision of both your community and your world and how we can make them better places for our children.

**Neal Hoffman, Past District Governor,
Santa Clara Rotary Club, Santa Clara, CA, USA**

Email: njhdds@ix.netcom.com

* * * * *

Rotary makes the phrase *The Human Family* real. It is an organization that looks past race, religion, and creed and makes us all a part of a universal human family.

The belief in *SERVICE ABOVE SELF* is an enduring and irresistible belief. It is a fundamental tenet of all religions and we chose our heroes in life because of it. From cartoon characters like Superman to real life people like Abraham Lincoln and Mahatma Gandhi—they were an embodiment of this ideal.

Charity begins at home but does not end there. Join Rotary to serve the world. Our world. A human world that can also be a humane world.

**Dr Siva Ananthan, Past Club President,
Damansara Rotary Club, Kuala Lumpur, Malaysia**

Email: inirwana@tm.net.my

* * * * *

Rotary is the one and only organization which can change people's lives. In service, I found Rotary the best. Over and above everything, Rotary is the best platform for developing one's leadership qualities. In 1992, as a new member, when I stood before the microphone to read the invocation, my legs were shivering and my body was sweating. Now I speak at district functions, train Rotarians during PETS and Assembly, and conduct seminars regularly for hundreds of people. Thanks to Rotary, I am proud to say that I am a Rotarian.

**K. Mohandas, Rotarian,
Rotary Club of Cochin South, Cochin, Kerala, India**

Email: expertec@vsnl.com

* * * * *

I entered the Service Club World for all the wrong reasons: mainly to increase my business by networking with the club members. This did not work so I prepared to quit. The man who sponsored me into the club told me to stick around but this time look to the club as an opportunity to serve humanity not myself. New as I was to this concept, I tried it—and low and behold, I started to really enjoy the service club. I made many new friends all the while using the club to do good works in our community and the world. I have been an active member now for 26 years. One of the most surprising benefits from Rotary, besides the gratitude and satisfaction of doing good works with good people, was the side benefit of peer group support. Many professional people surround themselves with employees or family that may not tell you what you need to hear. I have found that the friends I meet in Rotary, my peer group, will be more than happy to set me straight when I may stray from the course. An added benefit for sure. PS: My business did increase! Why? Maybe because of Rotary I changed and the customers liked it.

William Lee Reeves, Past District Governor,
Carson City Noon Rotary Club, Carson City, Nevada USA

Email: reeves@accutek.com

* * * * *

Join Rotary in order to give economical or practical help to suffering peoples around the world—a help, which will always reach the place where it is needed. Join Rotary to get into a friendship worldwide with all the facilities thereby. I know that I could never have met so many friends without Rotary.

Flemming Sørensen, District Governor,
Rotary Club of Faxe, Fakse, Denmark

Email: faas@post.tele.dk

* * * * *

I joined Rotary, because a businessman in town pressured me, even though I felt no need to join a club that was made up of mostly men. Going into my thirteenth year as a member of the Rotary club, the following is my testimony on why I hope to be a life member of Rotary!

The time of day you meet is not important, rather the people you will meet: most members possess the work ethics, family values, community commitment, and international concern for others that would make anyone proud to become a member of Rotary. The Four Way Test, for me is second only to the Ten Commandments. No matter what your beliefs, the Four Way Test contains the basic instructions necessary to bring our private life and the world closer towards meeting our goals for Peace if taken seriously. Rotary activities, actions, goals, and potential for new friends has added so much to my personal and business life, I can't imagine why people who are able to join Rotary, wouldn't run to the nearest club for membership.

**Joan E. Capurro, Rotarian,
Rotary Club of Ross Valley, San Anselmo, Calif. USA**

Email: joancapurro@bankofmarin.com

* * * * *

1) Where can you have friendship with so many different professions? Normally the friendship circles around the branch you are working in. 2) The view is enriched and broadened enormously through the many different professions. 3) As you have mutual targets to work for all together and you earn the success, it makes you proud and content to be a Rotarian.

**Kurt Timoschek, Past Club President,
Feldbach Rotary Club, Feldbach, Austria**

Email: kurt.timoschek@netway.at

* * * * *

In Hawaii, the word for family is 'ohana.' Rotary is my extended ohana. I am inspired, motivated and comforted by the wisdom and consistency of my Rotary family. Together we share fellowship, laugh, learn, and make a difference at home and beyond. Every member is unique, but each embraces a similar work ethic and passion for Service Above Self. My husband told me once, that he no longer frets about the statistical inevitability of his passing before I do. Because, he said, the Rotary ohana will be there for you, after I am gone.

Linda Coble, District Governor,
Rotary Club of Honolulu, Honolulu, Hawaii, USA

Email: k59linda@pixi.com

* * * * *

Rotary membership will help you grow spiritually, mentally, emotionally, socially, and financially. You will build lifelong friendships, and in time of trouble, illness, and stress, Rotary will provide you a support system. You will be educated on subjects you never would otherwise, and you will have the opportunity to meet and greet other peoples of the world. It will provide you the opportunity to serve, and to belong to an organization that includes in its membership everybody who is anybody. In fact, there are but a few organizations that can marshal the influence and leadership that Rotary represents. Being a Rotarian will just plain make you feel good.

Robert H. Pityo, Rotarian,
Rotary Club of Cedar Grove, Cedar Grove, NJ, USA

Email: Bbpityo@aol.com

* * * * *

Rotarians role model responsible citizenship in our community . . . and worldwide. Respect and cooperation help achieve projects that seem just a dream without everyone working together. Each Rotarian builds on the others' abilities and talents . . . to achieve projects seemingly impossible. Friendship in Rotary is an important factor, and is achieved internationally. Immediate acceptance of another Rotarian opens doors to friendship, travel, major projects, and long-term club associations. To me it is the most important ingredient in the recipe of success!

Philippa Follert, Past Club President,
Montrose Rotary Club, Montrose, Pa. U.S.A.

Email: pfollert@hotmail.com

* * * * *

My closest friends are from Rotary and this reason alone is enough to join Rotary. The added benefit is the opportunity to contribute to society to a much larger extent than what you can do individually. Holding offices in Rotary gives you the extra input in management capabilities which will help you in your own profession. Ultimately, what difference will be there between animals and us if we do not apply our resources in serving others? And no other organisation can give you such opportunites as Rotary.

R. Guru, Rotarian,
Rotary Club of Mysore, Mysore, Karnataka, India

Email: gurunrrs@vsnl.com

* * * * *

"Synergy" is the word that best describes my reason for first joining and for remaining in Rotary. I have always wanted to serve my community, but with a full-time job and businesses of my own, I hardly found the time. Through Rotary, I am able to combine my efforts with other Rotarians and the sum of the total effort far exceeds what each of us can do individually. In addition, the fellowship with like-minded peers, is just unbelievable, Come join us.

Wellington Johnson, Rotarian,
Rotary Club of West Nassau, Nassau, Bahamas

Email: wellie_johnson@excite.com

* * * * *

I wanted to be part of a community service organisation which had no religious or political affiliations, and I joined my Rotary club in 1989 when the RI theme was "Enjoy Rotary." I had so much fun with my new friends, who really knew how to do the serious work of serving the community with such a "joie de vivre," that I have never looked back.

Vince Pinto, Past Club President,
Rotary Club of Kowloon Golden Mile, Hong Kong

Email: pinto@selpro.com.hk

* * * * *

I was not a "joiner." Never thought I had time. Finally, I was invited to join Rotary and the time seemed right to give it a try. This was one of the best decisions I have ever made. I thoroughly enjoy the fellowship with the many good friends I have made. We have great fun working together on our many humanitarian projects. I take pride in being a part of an exemplary worldwide service organization.

John T. Smith, Past Club President,
Rotary Club of Ross Valley, San Anselmo, CA, USA

Email: jotsmith@yahoo.com

* * * * *

When I joined Rotary, I was unable to function well in front of large groups and I had a very small group of acquaintances to assist in my social development. I was eager to give something back to my community, but was only one. Today, I am able to speak in front of groups and leave an impact. I have friends all over the world whom I can call on for questions, assistance, guidance, and friendship. I have great pride for the work I am a part of, not only in my community, but around the world. Other than my family, Rotary has been the single most fulfilling experience of my life.

Barry Rassin, Past District Governor,
East Nassau Rotary Club, Nassau, Bahamas

Email: barryjras@yahoo.com

* * * * *

John F. Kennedy stated, "The making of peace is the noblest work of men." Rotary makes peace! We have stopped wars to inoculate children. We hold peace conferences. We feed the hungry, and provide clean water. We clothe the needy and provide medical care. Our exchange programs promote peace on a one-on- one basis—ROTARY MAKES PEACE!

Michael L. Browne, Past District Governor, Rotary Club
of Windsor-St.Clair, Windsor, Ontario, Canada

Email: governormike@hotmail.com

* * * * *

There were three main reasons for joining Rotary, I had already had a start as I was in Apex and the St John Ambulance Brigade, both community service-based organisations. I joined for fellowship, and I now have many Rotarian friends, both at home and internationally, to serve the community. When I was young, my Father impressed upon me the need to give back some of the good things that you have received. My third reason is the networking of Rotary, both personally and business. The ability to conduct business with people you know who hold the same ethical views as yourself is simply priceless.

Larry Jacka, Past District Governor, Rotary Club of West Pennant Hills, Sydney NSW Australia

Email: ljacka@zip.com.au

* * * * *

Rotary provides you with the company of enlightened leaders of your community. Rotary gives the opportunity to serve. Rotary gives you the opportunity to develop and polish your leadership abilities. Rotary makes you feel GREAT, and makes others happy through your work. Join Rotary and see a new world! Share Rotary with your friends!

Dr. Ali Akhtar, Past Club President, Rotary Club of Karachi Cosmopolitan, Karachi, Pakistan

Email: akhtar02@super.net.pk

* * * * *

Joining Rotary is an opportunity. And, like all opportunities, you will get out of it what you put in. When you join Rotary and participate fully, you will discover true fellowship and the joy that comes from serving your club, your community, and our world. You will receive more than you ever give, because the reward for service is in the knowledge that service has been given and that you have truly made a difference.

Joseph (Joe) F. LaGuess, District Governor, Rotary Club of Rancho Mirage, Rancho Mirage, Ca. USA

Email: jlaguess@earthlink.net

* * * * *

To join Rotary is to open up a door which you can step into, and there you will find a fantastic positive world of international contacts and fellowship. At the same time are you able to enjoy your "family" in the shape of your own small Rotary club in which you are a member. The spectra of everyone's background shows the strengths of the entire Rotary and gives this a special colour by the different individuals which are a link-up to a worldwide chain called Rotary International.

**Rolf Cederholm, Rotarian, Rotary Club
of Angelholm-Luntertun, Angelholm, Sweden
Email: rolf.cederholm@mail.bip.net**

* * * * *

Meeting with community business leaders weekly is very inspiring. New ideas are radiated, and this group's energy really does make things happen. Rotary offers an incredibly well-organized system of volunteers—each of whom do a little bit that collectively matters a lot. Since everybody participates in some way, we have a grand opportunity to get to know and appreciate each other.

**Dot Greene, District Governor,
Monroe Rotary Club, Monroe, North Carolina USA
Email: dotgreene@carolina.rr.com**

* * * * *

Share your expertise and be a force for good by serving your community. We offer you a unique opportunity to serve with Rotary. Together, we can extend more services to others. Get to expand your circle of friends and do your share in promoting world understanding and peace.

**Jaime Ramon M. Ortigas, Past Club President,
Rotary Club of San Juan, Metro Manila, Philippines
Email: j_ortigas@yahoo.com**

* * * * *

APPENDIX B

20 Answers to the Question: Why Join Rotary?

**by Richard D. King, President,
Rotary International, 2001-2002**

1. **Friendship:** In an increasingly complex world, Rotary provides one of the most basic human needs: the need for friendship and fellowship. It is one of two reasons why Rotary began in 1905.

2. **Business Development:** The second original reason for Rotary's beginning is business development. Everyone needs to network. Rotary consists of a cross section of every business community. Its members come from all walks of life. Rotarians help each other and collectively help others.

3. **Personal Growth and Development:** Membership in Rotary continues one's growth and education in human relations and personal development.

4. **Leadership Development:** Rotary is an organization of leaders and successful people. Serving in Rotary positions is like a college education. Leadership is learning how to motivate, influence and lead leaders.

5. **Citizenship in the Community:** Membership in a Rotary club makes one a better community citizen. The average Rotary club consists of the most active citizens of any community.

6. **Continuing Education:** Each week at Rotary there is a program designed to keep one informed about what is going on in the community, nation, and world. Each meeting provides an opportunity to listen to different speakers and a variety of timely topics.

7. **Fun:** Rotary is fun, a lot of fun. Each meeting is fun. The club projects are fun. Social activities are fun. The service is fun.

8. **Public Speaking Skills:** Many individuals who joined Rotary were afraid to speak in public. Rotary develops confidence and skill in public communication and the opportunity to practice and perfect these skills.

9. **Citizenship in the World:** Every Rotarian wears a pin that says "Rotary International." There are few places on the globe that do not have a Rotary club. Every Rotarian is welcome—even encouraged—to attend any of the 30,000 clubs in 199 nations and geographical regions. This means instant friends in both one's own community and in the world community.

10. **Assistance when Traveling:** Because there are Rotary clubs everywhere, many a Rotarian in need of a doctor, lawyer, hotel, dentist, advice, etc., while traveling has found assistance through Rotary.

11. **Entertainment:** Every Rotary club and district has parties and activities that provide diversion in one's business life. Rotary holds conferences, conventions, assemblies, and institutes that provide entertainment in addition to Rotary information, education, and service.

12. **The Development of Social Skills:** Every week and at various events and functions, Rotary develops one's personality, social skills and people skills. Rotary is for people who like people.

13. **Family Programs:** Rotary provides one of the world's largest youth exchange programs; high school and college clubs for future Rotarians; opportunities for spouse involvement; and a host of activities designed to help family members in growth and the development of family values.

14. **Vocational Skills:** Every Rotarian is expected to take part in the growth and development of his or her own profession or vocation; to serve on committees and to teach youth about one's job or vocation. Rotary helps to make one a better doctor, lawyer, teacher, etc.

15. **The Development of Ethics:** Rotarians practice a 4-Way Test that governs one's ethical standards. Rotarians are expected to be ethical in business and personal relationships.

16. **Cultural Awareness:** Around the world, practicality every religion, country, culture, race, creed, political persuasion, language, color, and ethnic identity is found in Rotary. It is a cross section of

the world's most prominent citizens from every background. Rotarians become aware of their cultures and learn to love and work with people everywhere. They become better citizens of their countries in the process.

17. **Prestige:** Rotary members are prominent people: leaders of business, the professions, art, government, sports, military, religion, and all disciplines. Rotary is the oldest and most prestigious service club in the world. Its ranks include executives, managers; professional people who make decisions and—influence policy.

18. **Nice People:** Rotarians above all are nice people— the nicest people on the face of the earth. They are important people who follow the policy: *it is nice to be important but it is important to be nice.*

19. **The Absence of an "Official Creed":** Rotary has no secret handshake, no secret policy, no official creed, no secret meeting or rituals. It is an open society of men and women who simply believe in helping others.

20. **The Opportunity to Serve:** Rotary is a service club. Its business is mankind. Its product is service. Rotarians provide community service to both local and international communities. This is perhaps the best reason for becoming a Rotarian: the chance to do something for somebody else and to sense the self-fulfillment that comes in the process and return of that satisfaction to one's own life. It is richly rewarding.

"He profits most who serves best."

Create Awareness — Take Action

Now it's up to you! Don't sit around wondering how it might have been, act today!

For more information on how to join Rotary, or to see where clubs meet, what activities Rotarians are involved in, go to either the official Rotary Website or my personal Website and let your fingers do the clicking! Look at what Rotarians are saying about their decision to join Rotary. Check out the Task Forces. Just browse from page to page—*and then take action!*

www.Rotary.org
www.FrankDevlyn.org

See you in Rotary!

—Frank Devlyn